HOW TO PREPARE A SCIENTIFIC DOCTORAL DISSERTATION BASED ON RESEARCH ARTICLES

The article-based thesis is becoming increasingly common, especially in the "hard" sciences such as biology, medicine, and technology, and is beginning to replace the traditional monograph. Format guidelines vary among universities. This is the first book to summarize the main features, showing the PhD student how to prepare a thesis in such a format.

The suggestions are highly practical; both the good and bad examples from published theses support the author's wise advice on all aspects of such theses. Poor figures are not only scrutinized in detail, but are also redrawn for comparison. Guidance also covers the issues of reprint permissions and copyright.

This informative and accessible book, by the author of *How to Write and Illustrate a Scientific Paper*, has developed through the author's extensive teaching experience in scientific writing and also through his experience as a journal editor. It is an indispensable guide to article-based thesis success.

BJÖRN GUSTAVII has been teaching courses in scientific writing for doctoral students for over 30 years. He brings his personal experience to this book, both from his work as a journal editor and from producing more than 100 of his own research papers. He is the author of the highly successful *How to Write and Illustrate a Scientific Paper* (2nd edition, Cambridge, 2008).

How to
Prepare a

Scientific Doctoral Dissertation Based on Research Articles

Björn Gustavii
Lund University, Sweden

CAMBRIDGE
UNIVERSITY PRESS

CAMBRIDGE UNIVERSITY PRESS
Cambridge, New York, Melbourne, Madrid, Cape Town,
Singapore, São Paulo, Delhi, Mexico City

Cambridge University Press
The Edinburgh Building, Cambridge CB2 8RU, UK

Published in the United States of America by Cambridge University Press, New York

www.cambridge.org
Information on this title: www.cambridge.org/9781107669048

First published 2012

Printed and bound in the United Kingdom by the MPG Books Group

A catalogue record for this publication is available from the British Library

Library of Congress Cataloging-in-Publication Data

Gustavii, Björn, 1932–
    How to prepare a scientific doctoral dissertation based on research articles / Björn Gustavii,
Lund University, Sweden.
        pages cm
    ISBN 978-1-107-66904-8 (Paperback)
    1. Dissertations, Academic–Handbooks, manuals, etc.   2. Science–Study and teaching
(Graduate)–Handbooks, manuals, etc.   I. Title.
    LB2369.G87 2012
    808.02–dc23

                                                                      2012017174

ISBN 978-1-107-66904-8 Paperback

Contents

Preface

Before writing this book, I looked into a couple of thousand theses[1] based on published (and ready-for-publication) papers. Most of them I viewed on the Internet, but several I surveyed while on location in various university libraries. Merely seeing an image of a thesis on the Internet is not the same as having a paper version in your hands; to smell and feel the paper – I love it!

Although the examples shown are real (if not otherwise stated), bad ones are given without revealing the source. When I wanted to include a figure, I sought permission from the author. If the example was bad, the author was informed of the changes suggested and of the form the credit line would take, for example: *Reproduced from a thesis published in 2008, with permission*. All the authors asked gave me permission. I am grateful for your generosity, which has provided the readers with authentic examples from which to learn. Thank you!

This book is about the overall summary of a thesis (also called the *overview*[2]). It is thus *not* about the research papers which were

---

[1] The terms *thesis* and *dissertation* are used differently in different parts of the world. For example, in the USA, master's students write *theses* whereas in Britain, they write *dissertations*. At the PhD level, however, these terms are reversed. In this book the terms *thesis* and *dissertation* are used interchangeably.

[2] *Overview*: To mention a few variants, this is also called *contextual statement, explanatory essay, linking narrative, summarizing report, integrating paper, cover story, frame* and *synthesis*.

dealt with in my book *How to Write and Illustrate a Scientific Paper* (2nd edition, Cambridge University Press, 2008). Such research papers authored by the degree candidate have passed editorial scrutiny; the overview has not. As a former editor of a scientific journal, I had the experience of giving this overview a closer look.

Björn Gustavii
bjorngustavii@telia.com

Acknowledgments

I thank the following persons, who read all or parts of the manuscript, for their advice and criticism.

Joy Burrough-Boenisch

Mikael Elofsson

Ulf Havelius

Martin Ingvar

Johan Ljungqvist

Gunilla Nordin Fredrikson

Kerstin Nilsson

Marju Orho-Melander

Amra Osmancevic

Stacey Ristinmaa-Sorensen

Kathryn L. Roberts

Stellan Sandler

Anita Sjölander

Gunnevi Sundelin

Lena Svedberg

Lil Träskman Bendz

Pål Wölner-Hanssen

Lena Zidén

Anna Åkerud

Special thanks to Tomas Söderblom, a layperson who read the manuscript for intelligibility; Carol Norris, who scrutinized the text; Richard Fisher, who corrected the language; and Ronny Lingstam and Åsa Jägergård, who remade the tables and redrew the graphs.

Finally – my thanks to Katrina Halliday, senior commissioning editor, Cambridge University Press, for her thorough revision of the manuscript.

1
Introduction

This book is about the overview of the article-based thesis. It is written for graduate students mainly in the "hard" sciences, such as biology, medicine, and technology. The best time to read this book would be when you are finishing your individual papers.

However, you must find out at an early stage whether your university allows you to use the article-based format. If not, you have to write a traditional monograph thesis. Then, the contents of this book would be helpful to you as well. Listed below are those parts that are also valid for the traditional monograph.

> Front cover picture
> Title
> Abstract
> Quotations
> Abbreviations
> Acknowledgment
> General introduction
> Aims

General discussion
Copyright

To a certain extent, the content of the methods and results sections could also prove beneficial.

2

Compilation – the article-based thesis

This chapter is a review of the article-based thesis, also called *compilation* thesis. The compilation is increasingly encouraged, especially in the hard sciences such as biology, medicine, and technology.

Compilations

Compilations are of two types. In one, the reprinted articles are appended to an overall summary of their content, here called the *Scandinavian model*. In the other, the reprinted articles are sandwiched between introductory and concluding chapters, here called the *sandwich format*.[1]

Scandinavian model

Common to theses of the Scandinavian model is that an overall summary (overview) is followed by research papers – bound together in a single volume. Published articles are reproduced as

---

[1] A *sandwich* refers to two slices of bread with a layer of food between them, named after the inventor, the fourth Earl of Sandwich (1718–1792).

exact copies of the articles as they appear in the publishing journal (including title pages with original letterheads, logotypes, typefaces, and so on) – in short, as reprints; papers *in press* are reproduced as preprints.

In contrast with the research papers, which are highly structured, the overview of the Scandinavian type of compilation has no formula for arranging its various parts, not even regarding which parts to include.

A basis for discussion

In this book I suggest a scheme (see *Contents*) based on real examples gathered from a large number of compilations of the Scandinavian model. This layout can serve as a basis for the discussion. I emphasize, however, that the sections could be rearranged, for example, *Acknowledgments*, the part most read, could be placed first, and some parts could be excluded, such as *Thesis at a glance* and *Contributors*, as appropriate locally.

Sandwich – the format used in the rest of the world

Outside Scandinavia, the most commonly used format for an article-based thesis worldwide is the sandwich. The articles appear as chapters between the general introduction and the general discussion. If the articles are published or accepted for publication, these chapters are usually the final version of the manuscript as sent to the journal (Figure 2.1).

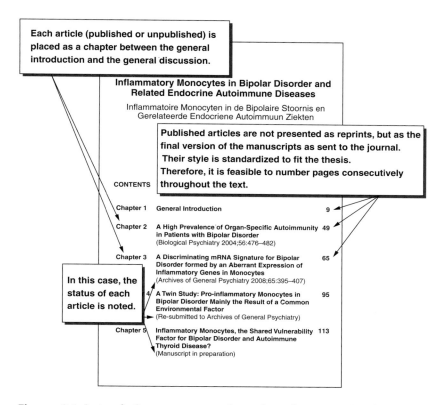

Figure 2.1 Part of the *contents* section of a thesis in the format of a sandwich. (Reproduced with permission from Roos Padmos, 2009, Erasmus University, the Netherlands.)

Illustrations

In the sandwich format, you can use part of the title page of each chapter as an illustration (Figure 2.2). The example is taken from a thesis at National University in Australia, where this format is called *thesis by publication* (Debra L. Saunders, 2008).

Figure 2.2 Each of six chapters of the thesis begins with a picture of the swift parrot and a pertinent citation, as in this title page. (Reproduced from Debra L. Saunders, 2008, with permission from the author and the painter, E. E. Gostelow.)

Sandwich format vs. Scandinavian model

The sandwich format and the Scandinavian model both have advantages. The sandwich format usually has the following benefits: (a) The articles (chapters) are standardized to fit the thesis, which makes it look like a book. (b) Parts of the title pages can serve as illustrations. In the Scandinavian model, your published articles appear as reprints, looking exactly as do the articles in the published journal, and giving the author a feeling of being in the midst of the scientific production. That is a great feeling.

Besides these differences, the content of the book itself is mainly applicable to both formats – if not otherwise stated. Well, now, let's begin.

3

Front cover illustration

A journalist from a daily newspaper was one of the teachers at a course on scientific writing. During a break she looked into a thesis overview. (At that time the overview was published separately from the research papers.) She paged through the publication and then said:

> Not a single illustration, not even a cover picture.

Still – about forty years later – in technology, a picture on a thesis cover is seldom seen, nor does one occur often in medicine. However, in biology, it has become the norm.

In biology, an animal studied does not need be camouflaged to be portrayed on the cover. In medicine, the need of disguising a patient studied is a problem. On the next page we have one example of how the problem could be solved – by showing the individual in silhouette (Figure 3.1).

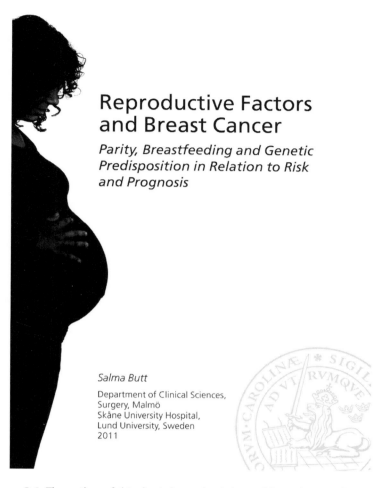

Reproductive Factors and Breast Cancer

Parity, Breastfeeding and Genetic Predisposition in Relation to Risk and Prognosis

Salma Butt

Department of Clinical Sciences,
Surgery, Malmö
Skåne University Hospital,
Lund University, Sweden
2011

Figure 3.1 The author of this thesis has solved the problem of camouflaging the pregnant woman by showing her in silhouette. Even her mother probably could not identify her. Of course, you must have her written permission.[1] This is a fine illustration of the subject of the thesis. (Reproduced with the permission of the author Salma Butt (2011), the designer Maria Näslund, Formfaktorn, and the photographer Thomas Prahl.)

---

[1] See Chapter 18, "Photo of a human being," Figure 18.3 and 18.4.

Instead of showing a patient on the cover, you can depict what symptoms a person has from the disease studied, as here (Figure 3.2):

Figure 3.2 Alzheimer's disease was the subject of this thesis. The cartoon speaks for itself in balloons. Note the error "take at [sic] short walk." (Reproduced from Sofia Holback (2009), with permission from the author and the artist, motorcycle policeman Stefan Andén, Popcop © 2008).

... or symbolically depict the topic of the thesis (Figure 3.3):

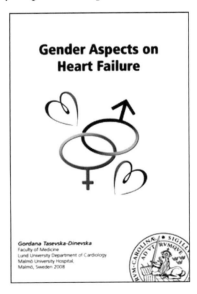

Figure 3.3 A symbolic drawing with reference to the subject studied. (Reproduced with permission from Gordana Tasevska-Dinevska, 2008)

... or illustrate how the treatment functions (Figure 3.4):

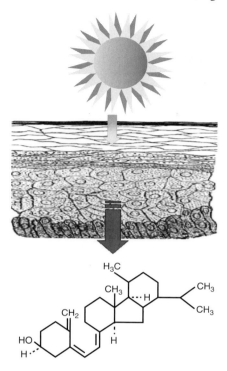

Figure 3.4 The sun shines on the skin resulting in the production of vitamin D, illustrating the subject of the thesis: Vitamin D status in psoriasis patients treated with UVB [ultraviolet B] therapy. (Reproduced with permission from Amra Osmancevic, 2009.)

In the legend, placed on one of the initial pages, the author explains what the illustration is meant to say, not only what it shows.

> The cover picture illustrates the sun, the skin compartments . . . and the chemical structure of vitamin D3. Ultraviolet . . . radiation stimulates the production of vitamin D3 in the stratum basale [a deep layer of the skin].

Do not forget to credit the person who made the illustration. If you yourself made it, say so, "The front cover picture drawn by me [not 'by the author']. The drawing shows . . . and is meant to say. . ."

However, in biology and technology, no ethical aspects usually have to be considered when putting, in pictorial form, the subject of the thesis on the front cover, as here (Figure 3.5):

Figure 3.5 A bird, like this one, does not care about having her portrait on the cover. In biology, a cover illustration seems to be the norm. (Reproduced with permission from Olle Lind, 2011.)

. . . or, as here (Figure 3.6):

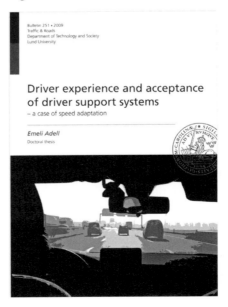

Figure 3.6 In technology, a cover illustration is surprisingly uncommon. Thereby, the author misses a fine opportunity to draw attention to the studies. This picture invites the reader to open the thesis. (Reproduced with permission from Emeli Adell, 2009.)

An approach that is always available is shown in Figure 3.7:

Figure 3.7 A picture like this can be made within seconds on the site *wordle.net* (as long as this service is still on the web; if not, you may find another similar service). You can, for example, take your thesis abstract or part of it and paste it into the appropriate box. If you have no suitable cover figure, this is better than nothing. (Reproduced with permission from Avinash Abhyankar, 2009.)

Figure 3.7 could be regarded as an exception to the rule in scientific writing of not using a picture for decoration only. This exception is valid, to a certain extent, also for the preceding illustrations of this chapter.

4

Title

The main title for the broad aspect and a subtitle for the details may be an effective title for your thesis. Thus, *not* like this:

Growth Hormone in Athletes

What was studied? The aim was not to study the normal value of the hormone, but to study markers to be used in forthcoming doping tests. You may inform the reader about that in a subtitle. (In the following, the main titles are in bold face.)

Growth Hormone in Athletes
Markers to be used in tests for doping

Here is a fine example of this type of title (Anna Wik, 2008):

When Rubber Meets the Road
Ecotoxicological Hazard and Risk Assessment of Tire Wear Particles

and here is another (Per Henningsson, 2010):

Always on the wing
Fluid dynamics, flight performance and flight behavior of common swifts

and another (Rahmat Naddafi, 2007):

Invasion of the Zebra Mussel
Effects on Phytoplankton Community Structure and Ecosystem Function

However, no subtitle is needed when the reader is informed of both the subject and what was done, as in the following example (Emma Sorbring, 2005):

Girls' and Boys' Views of Conflicts with Parents

or (David Lindström, 2008):

The Impact of Tobacco Use on Postoperative Complications

Begin with the keywords

Today, most scientists skim lists of titles on a computer screen. Hurried readers may not have the time to find the keywords if they occur somewhere in the middle or at the end of a title. Consider this title of a thesis,

Incidence, emergence, persistence and mechanisms of antimicrobial resistance in clinical isolates and normal microbiota

which could be changed to

Antimicrobial resistance
Incidence, emergence, persistence and mechanisms in clinical isolates and normal microbiota

Avoid abbreviations in the title

A title should contain no undefined abbreviations, like the following:

Shoulder instability
A clinical and MRI-based analysis

Write out MRI (Michael R. Torkzad, 2006):

Magnetic resonance imaging of the rectum
Diagnostic and therapy related aspects

Consider also this:

Adrenocorticolysis Induced by 3-MeSO$_2$-DDE
Mechanisms of Action, Kinetics and Species Differences

A non-specialist reader would not be helped by the written-out phrase of this abbreviation, i.e. 2-(4-chloro-3-methylsulphonylphenyl)-2-(4-chlorophenyl)-1,1-dichloroethane. However, as this substance is a DDT metabolite, the title will become easier to comprehend if this is stated as:

Adrenocorticolysis Induced by the DDT-metabolite 3-MeSO$_2$-DDE
Mechanisms of Action, Kinetics and Species Differences

In a title you can use abbreviations and symbols that are more familiar than the words they stand for, such as DDT, DNA, laser, and pH.

Titles ending with a question mark

A title of a thesis can very well be formulated as a question (Susanue Köbler, 2007):

Bilateral Hearing Aids for Bilaterally Hearing-Impaired Persons – Always the Best Choice?

Without a question mark this would actually be a declarative title (i.e. declaring the results of the study).

Neutral titles

In the *individual* paper you are encouraged to use a declarative title whenever possible. In such a paper, the title needs to cover only the results of one single aim. A thesis, however, has several aims, and a declarative title most often appears inappropriate. The following declarative title of a thesis is a poor one, especially because it is in the *present tense*, indicating that the issue is solved now and forever.

Resistin Is a Modulator of Inflammation and Autoimmunity

Maybe, more modestly:

Resistin as a Modulator of . . .

I have found only a few examples in which a declarative title works in a thesis. Here is one of them (Fazlul Karim, 2007):

Gender Matters
Understanding of access barriers to community-based tuberculosis care in Bangladesh

Thus, a declarative title may function occasionally, but, in general, you are advised not to use this type of title for your thesis.

Confusing titles

Consider this title of a thesis:

Angiogenic Response in the Hypoxic Heart
Experimental studies in mice

This title may, at first glance, confuse a reader outside the specialty. By reading the background you will find that the death rate from heart disease is lower among people living at high altitude, for example, at 4000 m above sea level in Peru, the reason being (it was speculated) that the reduced oxygen supply to the heart stimulates new vessel formation.

But what was done? Actually, hypoxia was first induced (by letting the mice live in chambers with reduced oxygen), before study of their angiogenic response. It would be easier to follow if the presentation was in that order.

Induced Hypoxia of the Heart in Mice
Angiogenetic response

Humor

Writing with humor is difficult. I will spare you bad examples from writers trying their hands at doing so. Instead, I would like to show you an example from a PhD candidate who succeeded in giving the title of his thesis a touch of humor (Hervé Kuendig, 2009):

Empty Glasses and Broken Bones
Epidemiological studies on alcohol and injuries treated at an emergency department in Switzerland

5

Abstract

By writing a *working* abstract at an early stage, you will provide yourself with a framework for the rest of the overview. This will guide you in deciding what to include and what to omit. Then, when you have completed the overview, you can return to the working abstract and recast it in its final form.

Unfortunately, there are those who write the abstract as their final effort, often in a hurry and without opportunity for reflection and revision. A tip: If you are pressed for time, and only then, you can use what you have already written. Take a red pencil and a ruler and underline relevant portions in the various sections; then, combine the underlined sentences into an abstract. The advantage of doing this is that you repeat what you have said previously, without having to use synonyms that can alter your original intention. Some people say that doing so is self-plagiarism. However, the sources from which you are repeating yourself are the very same research papers you are going to include in your bound thesis. These phrases have been formulated as precisely and clearly as you were able, so why should they be changed? Actually, there are journals that require you to compile your abstract in this manner. They have a point.

Most abstracts are unattractive because they are written as one single paragraph. Try to structure the abstract in a manner similar to that in the research papers. Bold-face the headings and put a blank line between the sections, as in the following way.

Background. [text]
Aims. [text]
Methods. [text]
Results. [text]
Discussion. [text]

Feel free to use whatever headings will suit your subject best. Two abstracts with an attractive layout are shown in Figures 5.1 and 5.2.

The opening sentence

The opening sentence of the abstract should catch the reader's eye, and not contain cumbersome words like this:

Synchronous fluorescence spectrophotometry (SFS) for benzo(*a*) pyrene-7,8-diol-9,10-epoxide (BPDE)-DNA was used to measure the *in vivo* and *in vitro* formed adducts in C57BL/6 (B6) and DBA/2 (D2) mice, responsive and nonresponsive, respectively.

The following opening is a good one (Sverker Ek, 1995):

The fetus as a patient is a challenge.

It is short, simple and also humorous – as the patient is an unborn offspring still in the womb.

Try to avoid abbreviations in the abstract

Abbreviations in the abstract must be clarified, because an abstract should be readable by itself as an entity separated from the rest of the text. Actually, in some cases the thesis abstract is still printed on a separate sheet which is inserted into the thesis.

Vitamin D status in psoriasis patients treated with UVB therapy

Department of Dermatology and Venereology, Institute of Clinical Sciences at Sahlgrenska Academy, University of Gothenburg, Göteborg, Sweden

Abstract

The thesis deals with the effect of ultraviolet B (UVB) 280–320 nm on vitamin D production in psoriasis patients during treatment with phototherapy.

Background: Psoriasis is a chronic, inflammatory disease affecting the skin and potentially the joints. Both genetic and environmental factors are important in the aetiology of the disease. Phototherapy (broadband UVB, narrowband UVB (NBUVB) and heliotherapy) is commonly used as treatment of psoriasis. Vitamin D3, or cholecalciferol, is produced in the basal epidermis by ultraviolet radiation (290–315 nm) of 7-dehydrocholesterol and hydroxylated in the liver to the major circulating metabolite 25-hydroxyvitamin D [25(OH)D]. Hydroxylation to 1,25-dihydroxyvitamin D [1,25(OH)2D] in the kidneys is stimulated by parathyroid hormone (PTH) and suppressed by phosphate. Sun exposure is the strongest factor influencing 25(OH)D.

Aims: 1) To study the effect of UVB on vitamin D synthesis in patients with psoriasis. 2) To examine possible differences between NBUVB and broadband UVB on vitamin D production in psoriatic patients. 3) To investigate the effect of UVB induced vitamin D on bone, lipid and carbohydrate status in psoriasis patients.

Methods: Serum 25(OH)D, 1,25(OH)2D, PTH, calcium and creatinine were measured before and after the phototherapy in white, Caucasian patients with active plaque psoriasis. Bone mineral density (BMD) was examined using Dual-Energy X-ray Absorptiometry (DEXA) in postmenopausal women with psoriasis. Lipid and carbohydrate status were assessed in patients treated with heliotherapy.

Results: Psoriasis improved in all patients, with a 75% reduction in PASI (Psoriasis Area and Severity Index) score on all regimes. Serum 25(OH)D increased and PTH decreased after phototherapy. The increase in 25(OH)D was higher in the broadband treated patients compared with NBUVB. There was no correlation between the dose of UVB and the increase of 25(OH)D. Postmenopausal women with psoriasis had higher BMD both at the hip and at the lumbar spine than age-matched controls. The ratio of low-density lipoprotein (LDL) and high-density lipoprotein cholesterol (HDL), and the levels of glycosylated haemoglobin A1c (HbA1c) decreased during heliotherapy.

Conclusion: UVB and heliotherapy increased the serum 25(OH)D production, reduced the serum PTH concentrations and improved psoriasis, lipid and carbohydrate status in the patients. Vitamin D production in psoriasis patients increased less with NBUVB than with broadband UVB phototherapy. Postmenopausa women with psoriasis had higher BMD than age-matched controls, a finding that could be related to their higher body weight, physical activity and the UVB exposure.

Key words: Vitamin D, PTH, psoriasis, bone mineral density, ultraviolet UVB
ISBN-978-91-628-7682-1
Göteborg 2009

Figure 5.1 The above overview abstract has conventional subheadings similar to those used in the individual papers. Although the layout of this abstract is fine, some of its abbreviations are not used in the rest of the abstract, such as DEXA, LDL, HDL, and HBA1c. So, why introduce these abbreviations? (Reproduced from a thesis published in 2009, with permission.)

Figure 5.2 The next page shows an abstract with an unconventional layout, written in plain words and without abbreviations other than CP (cerebral palsy), which is generally accepted (Lena Svedberg, 2009, with permission).

COLD FEET IN CHILDREN WITH NEUROLOGICAL DISORDERS

Lena Svedberg

Institute of Neuroscience and Physiology, Clinical Neuroscience and Rehabilitation, Sahlgrenska Academy, University of Gothenburg, Gothenburg, Sweden, 2009.

ABSTRACT

These studies focused on the presence of cold feet in children with neurological disorders and raised the questions: Does acupuncture affect skin temperature? Are cold feet a general symptom in children with neurological disorders? Are cold feet associated with other symptoms? What are the moods, health, and daily life experiences of these children's parents?

Study I assessed effects of acupuncture on skin temperature in children with neurological disorders. The study was of a pilot character, to determine if further investigation in a larger, well-characterised group could be worthwhile.

Study II analysed skin temperature variation between pre-school children with and without neurological disorders to determine if skin temperature and walking ability were correlated.

Study III investigated accompanying symptoms, such as cold extremities, constipation, pain, sleeping disorders, and well-being, and their treatment to determine *(i)* whether cold extremities is a general problem, *(ii)* what symptom treatment the children had received, *(iii)* associations between cold extremities and gross-motor function, and *(iv)* associations between cold extremities and other symptoms shown by the child.

Study IV described mood, health, and daily life experiences of the children's parents to investigate *(i)* impact that the child's impairments and symptoms have on the family and *(ii)* community services support.

Study I (single subject design; each child was its own control) comprised 6 children with neurological disorders. Study II (hypothesis refinement study) comprised 25 healthy children recruited from a community pre-school and 15 children with cerebral or spinal cord disorders from Child and youth neurohabilitation in Örnsköldsvik. Studies III and IV (postal survey, descriptive hypothesis-generating studies) comprised 107 children with cerebral palsy (Study III) and parents of 106 of these (Study IV) from 8 habilitation centres in the northern region of Sweden.

Conclusions:
• Acupuncture may increase skin temperature in some children with neurological disorders and cold extremities.
• Non-walking children with cerebral damage had significantly lower mean hand and foot skin temperature than did healthy controls.
• Of the 5 symptoms – cold extremities, pain, sleeping disorders, constipation, and impaired well-being – (i) most of the children with CP had had 1 or several symptoms for more than 1 year and (ii) symptom frequency was generally higher in non-walking children than in walkers. Of the children who had symptoms for more than 1 year, a surprisingly large number had received no treatment for them.
• Care-giving for a child with CP may affect parents' moods, health, and daily living – especially if the child has several impairments and symptoms. Frequent parental anxiety regarding the child's physical and psychological health might be associated with affected parental health.

Key words: Skin temperature/Acupuncture/Autonomic dysfunction/Cerebral palsy/Spinal cord disorder/Pain/Constipation/Sleeping disorders/Well-being/ Parental health/Parental mood/Restricted time/Services Support

ISBN 978-91-628-7856-6

6

Quotations

Quotations from famous individuals such as Socrates, Leonardo da Vinci and Charles Darwin occasionally appear on one of the opening pages before the text itself. However, what these people said seems to have less to do with the content of the thesis than to express more general views of research work, like the following popular one:

> Everything should be as simple as it can be, yet no simpler.
> — Albert Einstein

I have only found one citation that illustrated the essence of the actual findings, formulated by the graduate student himself (Adad Baranto, 2005).

> Too much or too little physical activity is equally harmful to the spine.
> — Adad Baranto

Try to avoid citing someone, unless the quotation is exactly to the point with respect to your subject.

7
Thesis at a glance

Thesis at a glance first appeared in a thesis by Elke Theander in 2005, at Lund University (Figure 7.3). Although this section has become popular in the local region, it has not yet – in 2011 – been recognized at other universities.

A *Thesis at a glance* could be described as an abstract of the abstracts and is extremely helpful to the reader. However, avoid including drawings, graphs, or tables in the one-page variant. They will be reduced too much to be readable (Figure 7.1). If you really need illustrations, you may want to use *two* pages, where pictures and tables can be made large enough to be legible (Figure 7.3). In the two-page variant, the pages should face each other, to allow readers to see the content at a glance.

No instructions for writing a *Thesis at a glance* exist. Its layout depends on the subject and the results obtained. On the following pages you will find four examples of *Thesis at a glance*. They are illustrative with respect to the layout.

Thesis at a Glance

Paper	Objective	Method	Illustration	Main findings / conclusion
Paper I **High frequency of contact allergy to gold in patients with endovascular coronary stents**	To explore whether there is over-representation of contact allergy to metals used in stents	A retrospective, cross-sectional study of 484 coronary stented patients using 437 dermatitis patients as controls		Indication of the possible sensitization of the coronary vessel by Au stents. Ni stents and Au stents should not be ruled out as risk factors for induction of contact allergy to these metals.
Paper II **Unexpected sensitization routes and general frequency of contact allergies in an elderly stented Swedish population**	To investigate contact allergies, apart from metals, in a stented population	A retrospective, cross-sectional study of 484 coronary stented patients using 437 dermatitis patients as controls		Contact allergy to non-metal sensitizers is common in an elderly Swedish stent population, although substantially less than in a dermatitis population. The findings indicate the importance of the oral mucosa in sensitization.
Paper III **A correlation found between contact allergy to stent material and restenosis of the coronary arteries**	To investigate possible relationships between stent material, contact allergy and restenosis	A retrospective study of 484 coronary stented patients		Contact allergy to the stent material gold, may increase the inflammatory reaction and thereby the risk of restenosis. A correlation was found between gold-plated stents, contact allergy to gold and an increased frequency of restenosis.
Paper IV **A correlation found between gold concentration in blood and patch test reactions in patients with coronary stents**	To investigate the gold and nickel release from stainless steel stents with and without gold plating	200 blood samples from patients with either Au or Ni stents in their coronary vessels		Gold is released from the Au stents and patients with a gold stent have a 5-fold higher B-Au than patients with a nickel stent. The patch test reactions to gold were correlated with B-Au: the higher B-Au, the stronger the patch test reaction.
Paper V **Does gold concentration in blood influence the result of patch testing to gold?**	To further investigate the correlation between B-Au and the result of patch testing to gold	A double-blind, placebo-controlled cross-over study of 24 dermatitis patients with contact allergy to gold		B-Au was higher after gold provocation whereas no treatment effect were discerned. Significant differences in period effect were observed. There was a correlation between B-Au and MEC; the higher B-Au, the lower MEC, indicating that the B-Au level is of importance for the skin reactivity to gold.

Au, gold; Ni, nickle; B-Au, gold concentration in blood;; MEC, minimal eliciting concentration

Figure 7.1 A one-page *Thesis at a glance*. Although otherwise well executed, the drawing and the graphs have been reduced too much to be legible – an outcome often seen in the one-page type. (*Stent* denotes a device used to hold a heart artery open after the vessel has been dilated by a balloon.) (Susanne Ekqvist, 2008, with permission.)

Thesis at a glance

Participants	People with Parkinson's disease (PD) who were either selected for, or treated with, bilateral Deep Brain Stimulation in the subthalamic nuclei (STN).
Study I	**31 participants**
Aim	To investigate how balance performance responded to STN stimulation when tested without anti-PD medication.
Methods	Tests were conducted without anti-PD medication (i.e., overnight withdrawal) at 6 and 12 months after surgery. The Berg balance scale & "the postural stability test" (Item 30, UPDRS III) were assessed both with the STN stimulation turned off and on.
Results	Both at 6 and 12 months, the results of the Berg balance scale & Item 30 were statistically improved when the STN stimulation was turned on.
Conclusions	When tested without anti-PD medication, STN stimulation improves functional balance performance and "postural stability".
Study II	**28 participants**
Aim	To investigate if balance performance was affected by long-term treatment of STN stimulation.
Methods	The Berg balance scale was assessed before as well as 1 and 3 years after surgery: with and without anti-PD medication and STN stimulation turned off and on.
Results	Without any treatment (no medication & stimulation turned off), the scores of the Berg balance scale aggravated over time. Three years after surgery, the scores still improved when turning the stimulation on. Anti-PD medication added to this effect.
Conclusions	Although balance performance decreased over time, functional balance performance was positively affected by STN stimulation. Anti-PD medication added to this effect.
Study III	**10 participants**
Aim	To explore the effect of STN stimulation on balance performance as assessed with clinical performance tests, posturography and subjective ratings of fear of falling.
Methods	Testing was conducted without anti-PD medication, and with the STN stimulation turned off and on (start randomized).
Results	STN stimulation improved (statistically) the results of all clinical tests, except sharpened Romberg. The subjective ratings showed an increased fall-related self-efficacy. Three participants did not manage posturography when the STN stimulation was turned off, but all did so when it was turned on. The posturography results of the seven participants with complete data showed no significant differences, but it may be caused by the small sample size.
Conclusions	In this sample, STN stimulation alone significantly improved the results of the clinical performance tests that mimic activities in daily living. This improvement was further supported by the patients' ratings of fear of falling, which was less severe with the STN stimulation turned ON. The posturography results of the seven participants with complete data showed no significant differences due to STN stimulation.
Study IV	**20 participants**
Aim	To explore how fear of falling and falls were affected one year after surgery.
Methods	Fear of falling was evaluated with questionnaires- before and one year after surgery. Falls were prospectively recorded (fall diary) both before and after surgery.
Results	One year after surgery, the participants rated themselves as having a lower activity avoidance and having an increased fall-related self-efficacy in more complex activities. The fall rate showed no significant difference.
Conclusions	After surgery, the scores that related to fear of falling showed improvements which indicate positive effects on activities and participation. This study can not support any change in fall rate after surgery, which could be caused by the small sample size. Further studies are warranted.

Figure 7.2 In this fine one-page variant of a *Thesis at a glance*, the space is too cramped to allow illustrations. (Reproduced with permission from Maria H. Nilsson, 2009, Department of Health Sciences, Lund University.)

(a)

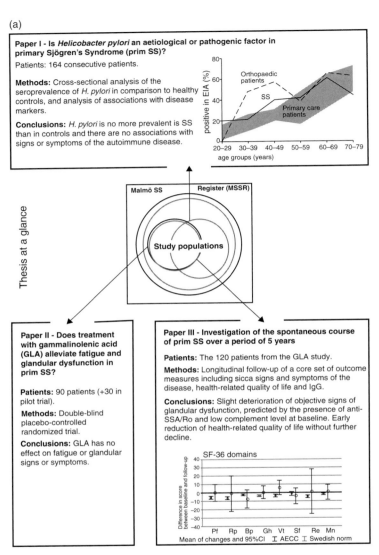

Paper I - Is *Helicobacter pylori* an aetiological or pathogenic factor in primary Sjögren's Syndrome (prim SS)?

Patients: 164 consecutive patients.

Methods: Cross-sectional analysis of the seroprevalence of *H. pylori* in comparison to healthy controls, and analysis of associations with disease markers.

Conclusions: *H. pylori* is no more prevalent is SS than in controls and there are no associations with signs or symptoms of the autoimmune disease.

Thesis at a glance

Malmö SS   Register (MSSR)

Study populations

Paper II - Does treatment with gammalinolenic acid (GLA) alleviate fatigue and glandular dysfunction in prim SS?

Patients: 90 patients (+30 in pilot trial).

Methods: Double-blind placebo-controlled randomized trial.

Conclusions: GLA has no effect on fatigue or glandular signs or symptoms.

Paper III - Investigation of the spontaneous course of prim SS over a period of 5 years

Patients: The 120 patients from the GLA study.

Methods: Longitudinal follow-up of a core set of outcome measures including sicca signs and symptoms of the disease, health-related quality of life and IgG.

Conclusions: Slight deterioration of objective signs of glandular dysfunction, predicted by the presence of anti-SSA/Ro and low complement level at baseline. Early reduction of health-related quality of life without further decline.

Figure 7.3 This is the pioneering work by Elke Theander (2005): the very first *Thesis at a glance*. It occupies two pages, so the space allows readable illustrations. (Elke Theander, 2005, with permission.)

(b)

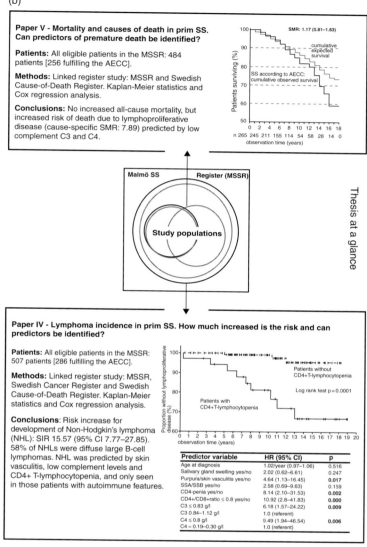

Paper V - Mortality and causes of death in prim SS. Can predictors of premature death be identified?

Patients: All eligible patients in the MSSR: 484 patients [256 fulfilling the AECC].

Methods: Linked register study: MSSR and Swedish Cause-of-Death Register. Kaplan-Meier statistics and Cox regression analysis.

Conclusions: No increased all-cause mortality, but increased risk of death due to lymphoproliferative disease (cause-specific SMR: 7.89) predicted by low complement C3 and C4.

Paper IV - Lymphoma incidence in prim SS. How much increased is the risk and can predictors be identified?

Patients: All eligible patients in the MSSR: 507 patients [286 fulfilling the AECC].

Methods: Linked register study: MSSR, Swedish Cancer Register and Swedish Cause-of-Death Register. Kaplan-Meier statistics and Cox regression analysis.

Conclusions: Risk increase for development of Non-Hodgkin's lymphoma (NHL): SIR 15.57 (95% CI 7.77–27.85). 58% of NHLs were diffuse large B-cell lymphomas. NHL was predicted by skin vasculitis, low complement levels and CD4+ T-lymphocytopenia, and only seen in those patients with autoimmune features.

Predictor variable	HR (95% CI)	p
Age at diagnosis	1.02/year (0.97–1.06)	0.516
Salivary gland swelling yes/no	2.02 (0.62–6.61)	0.247
Purpura/skin vasculitis yes/no	4.64 (1.13–16.45)	0.017
SSA/SSB yes/no	2.58 (0.69–9.63)	0.159
CD4-penia yes/no	8.14 (2.10–31.53)	0.002
CD4+/CD8+ratio ≤ 0.8 yes/no	10.92 (2.8–41.83)	0.000
C3 ≤ 0.83 g/l	6.18 (1.57–24.22)	0.009
C3 0.84–1.12 g/l	1.0 (referent)	
C4 ≤ 0.8 g/l	9.49 (1.94–46.54)	0.006
C4 = 0.19–0.30 g/l	1.0 (referent)	

Figure 7.3 (cont.)

THESIS AT A GLANCE

Paper I

Aim: Compare the clinical outcomes after surgical carpal tunnel release in diabetic and nondiabetic patients

Method: Patients were examined independently, by the same occupational therapist, prior to and 6, 12 and 52 weeks after surgery.

Evaluation methods: Sensory function (Semmes-Weinstein and static two-point discrimination test). Motor function (abductor pollicis brevis muscle strength, grip strength,key- and lateral-pinch). Pillar pain, scar allodynia, cold intolerance and patient satisfaction.

> **Conclusion:** Patients with diabetes have the same beneficial outcome after surgical carpal tunnel release as non-diabetic patients. Only cold intolerance was relieved to a lesser extent in the diabetic patients.

Paper II

Aim: Assess health-related quality of life (HRQL) in diabetic and non-diabetic patients with carpal tunnel syndrome.

Method: Preoperatively, 6, 12 and 52 weeks after surgical carpal tunnel release outcome questionnaires were administered to the patients.

Evaluation methods: Medical Outcomes Short-Form 36 Health Survey (SF-36) and diseasespecific Boston Carpal Tunnel Questionnaire (BTCQ). SF-36 population norms obtained from the Swedish database for population norms.

> **Conclusion:** Generic HRQL is impaired in diabetic patients with carpal tunnel syndrome (CTS) compared to non-diabetic patients with CTS and population norms. However, diabetic patients experience similar disease-specific, symptomatic and functional improvements after carpal tunnel release as non-diabetic patients.

Paper III

Aim: Describe nerve conduction results prior to and after carpal tunnel release in diabetic and non-diabetic patients.

Method: Nerve conduction studies were performed preoperatively and at the 52 weeks follow-up.

Evaluation methods: Median and ulnar nerve, distal motor latency, motor conduction velocity, compound muscle action potential, orthodromic sensory conduction velocity and action potentials. Median nerve, antidromic sensory conduction velocity across the carpal tunnel segment. Sural and peroneal nerve measurements to diagnose peripheral neuropathy.

> **Conclusion:** Marked neurophysiologic impairment or signs of peripheral neuropathy does not preclude significant recovery after carpal tunnel release in diabetic patients.

Figure 7.4 Another two-page variant of *Thesis at a glance*. The author has chosen to put frames around the most significant parts, the conclusions. (Reproduced from a thesis published in 2009, with permission.)

Paper IV

Aim: Evaluate if quantification of intraepidermal nerve fibre density (IENFD) at wrist level can detect signs of subclinical small nerve fibre neuropathy in diabetic patients.

Method: Punch biopsies from glabrous and hairy skin at wrist level were obtained in conjunction with surgical carpal tunnel release.

Evaluation methods: Biopsies immunostained with anti-protein gene product 9.5. The IENFD was quantified using manual counting by light microscopy.

Conclusion: At wrist level, IENFD is not different between diabetic and non-diabetic patients. However, IENFD was higher in females and more abundant in hairy compared to glabrous skin

Paper V

Aim: Establish if biopsy of the posterior interosseous nerve (PIN) at wrist level would be a feasible and low morbidity method to assess neuropathy in the forearm.

Method: PIN biopsy was performed on Type 2 diabetic subjects and compared to postmortem samples with no history of diabetes, carpal tunnel syndrome or neuropathy.

Evaluation methods: Light microscopy and digital imaging to measure fascicular area, myelinated nerve fibre density, endoneurial capillary density and subperineurial space.

Conclusion: The PIN biopsy procedure fulfils the criteria for nerve biopsy and is well tolerated by the patients. A reduction in myelinated nerve fibre density was demonstrated in diabetic patients.

Paper VI

Aim: Compare pathology in the non-compressed posterior interosseous nerve (PIN) between diabetic and non-diabetic patients with carpal tunnel syndrome.

Method: PIN biopsy was performed in conjunction with surgical carpal tunnel release. As a comparator we used PIN biopsies from subjects with no history of diabetes, carpal tunnel syndrome or neuropathy (post-mortem and biopsy samples taken during elective wrist surgery).

Evaluation methods: Light microscopy and digital imaging to measure fascicular area, myelinated nerve fibre density, endoneurial capillary density and subperineurial space.

Conclusion: Reduction in myelinated nerve fibre and capillary densities may predispose patients to carpal tunnel syndrome and this is further accentuated in diabetes.

Although the layout of this *Thesis at a glance* (Figure 7.4) is fine, the text contains unnecessary abbreviations.

Paper II: BTCQ, denoting Boston Carpal Tunnel Questionnaire, does not come up in the rest of the text. This abbreviation is not needed. CTS, denoting carpal tunnel syndrome, reappears once, where the short form can be replaced by "this syndrome."

Paper IV: IENFD, denoting intraepidermal nerve fiber density, can be replaced by "fiber density" or just "density."

Papers V and VI: PIN, denoting posterior interosseous nerve, appears four times and can be removed in each case. Instead of writing the "PIN biopsy," the "biopsy" alone suffices.

There is no reason to force the reader to memorize these short forms to be able to comprehend this section of a mere two pages. But, even worse, too often the short forms are undefined. The meaning of *at a glance* is lost, because the List of Abbreviations has to be consulted.

8

Abbreviations

In the thesis overview, abbreviations are often defined in a list (headed: "Abbreviations used") and also in the text when they first occur. Nevertheless, you should redefine them in the aims section.

Abbreviations in the aims section

In the aims section readers are often bombarded with undefined forms of abbreviations. Redefine them, as in this example (Raimo A. Lahti, 2005).

> [To assess the] use of autopsy in male deaths due to ischemic heart disease (IHD), in relation to all natural deaths (ND) and to cerebro-vascular deaths (CVD), as a determinant of the validity and reliability of cause-of-death (COD) statistics.

The cumbersome abbreviation

Try to replace a long and cumbersome abbreviation with a reader-friendly substitute. In one thesis the subject was hereditary non-polyposis colorectal cancer. The accepted abbreviation, HNPCC, was used frequently throughout the thesis. However, the list of abbreviations tells us that *Lynche syndrome* is synonymous with

HNPCC. So, as a non-specialist, I suggested in my course on scientific writing that the abbreviation could have been replaced with *Lynche syndrome*; alternatively with *the/this syndrome*. How much easier the text would have been to read with such a substitute.

However, in my May 2011 course, one participant (apparently an HNPCC expert) said that *Lynche syndrome* is no longer in use. So, to correct myself, instead of the words for this syndrome, you can use, for example, *this type of cancer* or *the cancer form studied* or just *the/this cancer*.

Unnecessary abbreviations

LA for left atrium, CS for caesarean section, AF for amniotic fluid or annulus fibrosus and even PD for Parkinson's disease are all abbreviations accepted in the specialty. However, just because an abbreviation is permitted does not mean that you are obliged to use it – especially not in a thesis overview which is written for the non-specialist.

9

List of publications

List of publications is intended to cover both published manuscripts (articles) and unpublished ones (papers).

Normally, you do *not* have the copyright to your own publications and must seek permission from the publishers to reproduce them. As some publishers are probably unaware of compilations, you have to inform them. The following example is fictitious.

> To the Publisher:
> I am preparing my doctoral (PhD) thesis, which is intended to be a compilation of an overall summary (overview) and research papers – bound together.
>
> I would greatly appreciate your permission to include:
>
> Andersson A, Pettersson, P. Smoking as a risk factor for cancer of the lungs. Journal of Significant Results, 2011;12:34–56.
>
> I would also like your permission to use Figure 1 from this article in my overview of the thesis.
> Yours sincerely,

The reference figures (2011;12:34–56) may be changed to *in press*, as appropriate. If the publisher has no electronic form to fill out, you may send the letter directly to the permissions department of the publisher; you will find the email address on the journal's homepage. If the publisher has its own permissions form (most publishers have), you may use it, of course. However, you are advised to paste the above permission letter into the appropriate box – so that all details are included, for example, the permission to use Figure 1.

Credit line

The credit line is usually placed at the bottom of the page that lists the individual papers. In such a line, some illogical writing may occur. Here is one example.

> All papers are reprinted with permission of the publishers.

One paper was *in press* and could not be *re*printed, only printed. Another paper was *submitted* and the author still had the copyright to this paper. The publishers were not named; they would probably have appreciated seeing their names in print, as they usually are when they give permission. The author of the following lines has formulated the credit line properly (Carin Staland Nyman, 2008).

> Paper I is **reprinted** by permission of SAGE Journals © 2008.
> Paper IV is **printed** by permission of WORK: A Journal of Prevention, Assessment and Rehabilitation. [Emphasis added.]

Paper I was published, whereas paper IV was only *in press*.

If a paper is submitted but not yet accepted, do not name the journal. Thus, "to *Journal of Cleaner Production*" should be deleted in the following example.

> Paper V. [names of authors]
>   [title of the paper]
>   Submitted ~~to Journal of Cleaner Production~~

The reason is that the journal can refuse publication (specialist journals refuse roughly half the papers submitted; certain general journals, such as *The Lancet*, over 95%). A colleague of mine, when applying unsuccessfully for a job, wrote in his CV (curriculum vitae) that he had submitted his latest papers to *The Lancet* – which eventually refused them all. When he applied for a similar job some years later, one of the referees, in his written review, asked what had happened to all those papers submitted to *The Lancet*.

In open-access journals, the authors retain the copyright. In a *List of publications*, the following statement was linked through an asterisk to Paper I (Inger Hallberg, 2009).

*Open access journal, authors retain copyright.

Within a few years, the last three words, *authors retain copyright*, will probably be superfluous.

A tip

Why not place the credit line immediately under the reference to which it belongs? If you do, it will become much easier to get it right (Rikard Nelander, 2009):

1. Rikard Nelander, [names of coauthors]
   [title of the paper]
   Journal of Applied Physics **102** 113104 (2007)
   ©2007 American Institute of Physics. Reprinted with permission.

Additional merits

If you have written a letter to the editor or a short report, which was based on your thesis research, you are strongly encouraged to include this letter or report in your *List of publications*. Such a report highlights your findings as being of immediate interest, and also shows that you have mastered the craft of writing concisely.

I remember an oral examination in which the graduate student in his thesis had not cited the most relevant work that had actually created his field of research. A person in the audience, a distinguished researcher, asked for permission to speak, *ex auditorio*. He asked the PhD candidate if he had read this publication and, if so, why he had not cited it. The graduate student answered, "Yes, I have read it, but not cited it, because it was only a letter." Actually, the content of a research letter can be more valuable than that of an original paper. A classic example is the short report by Watson and Crick (1953) on the structure of DNA, which occupies just over one page in *Nature*.

About referring

In the short publications mentioned above, the number of references is usually restricted; some journals allow only two. In such cases, if you need to quote more than two papers, you can do that by referring to a review article that includes them. But then, it could happen that the author of the review has not contributed to these findings, yet appears to get "credit" for them. This problem, however, apparently cannot be solved in another manner.

I take the opportunity here to say some some words about what to include in a reference list. When established researchers, such as the examiner of your thesis, scrutinize your papers, they often begin with the reference list. There they can get a good understanding of whether you have sound judgment on the subject you have chosen to study. The examiner, as an expert on the subject, knows exactly which are the key works and which are the "rotten works" (those below standard). The examiner can see at a glance whether you are a discerning person. So choose your references with care, and try not to include all your previous (say) nine publications in the list of every individual paper.

Errata

An author of one thesis had received faulty information from the National Office of Statistics about how often the condition she studied occurred. When she discovered this, the paper was already *in press* and she had to publish an erratum in a later issue of the journal. The erratum was included among the list of papers in the overview, like this (Elinor Ljungberg, 2008):

1. Ljungberg E, [names of coauthors]
   [title of paper]
   J Hand Surg 28B: 376–80, 2003.
   Erratum in: J Hand Surg 29B: 642, 2004. [Emphasis added.]

Tackling the problem in this manner would improve the credibility of her study.

10
Contributors

If papers included in your thesis have several authors, you must indicate which portions of the papers are your own work and which are the work of your co-workers. Some universities require that all authors sign a statement of their contribution. In other universities, especially in Scandinavia, the candidates themselves write a contribution list stating what each person did, as described in the following.

Every research project is divided into four main parts: designing the project, collecting the material, analyzing the results, and writing the paper. Because writing the paper is a major intellectual part of the research work, it is what counts most in the eyes of the examiner at the oral defense of a thesis.

Some graduate students have not written all the individual papers on their own – or, even worse, written none of them. They may indicate their contribution to the writing in different ways. Consider this:

I.   The author ... wrote **most** of the manuscript.
II. The author ... wrote **a major part** of the manuscript.
III. The author ... **assisted** in writing the manuscript.
IV. The author wrote **a significant part** of the manuscript.

V. The author . . . wrote **a substantial part** of the manuscript. [Emphasis added.]

The only thing we know for certain about this graduate student's contribution to the writing is that he has not authored one single paper in full. Consider:

Paper I: I wrote **most** of the paper (**90%**) . . .
Paper III: I wrote **most** of the paper (**75%**) . . . [Emphasis added.]

These statements, as well as those in the preceding paragraph, say nothing, if you do not indicate what sections you have written. Was it the methodology, which can be taken and reformulated (rephrased) from other people's publications? Or was it the discussion section – the heart of the paper?

I recommend that you yourself write the very first draft of your very first paper. It may be hard work, but to postpone writing on your own until the third or fourth paper will make it almost as painful. When you have written one paper, this rather quickly becomes easier for each paper. When you have finished your first draft, show it to your supervisor. If you are a first-time writer, the supervisor may have to revise your manuscript several times. As supervisors are aware that these multiple revisions may be necessary, they may offer the graduate student a joint co-authorship from the beginning. Resist the temptation to accept such an offer. (Your first draft will eventually be revised anyway by the supervisor, who is then usually included in the author by-line.) Try to make your contributors' list look as fine as this (Anders Vinther, 2009):

Study I

Study idea	Anders Vinther
Study design	Anders Vinther, [contributors]
Data collection	Anders Vinther, [contributors]
Data analysis	Anders Vinther, [contributors]
Manuscript writing	Anders Vinther
Manuscript revision	[contributors]

Study II . . .

Manuscript writing thus denotes writing the first draft. The list also includes *Study idea* as its first point. This is a good idea, but after years of research work it may be difficult to point out a particular person as a source for each paper – unless you wrote down the name when the idea first came up.

Most research nowadays is performed by groups. But if yours is a group of, say, three people, no list of contributors is needed. Instead, you can indicate what you did in this manner (Helena Berglund, 2009):

> My contribution to the papers:
> I have developed the ideas in cooperation with my [two] co-authors, suggested approaches to deal with database and statistical issues, performed the analysis, and written the first draft of all papers included.

One participant in one of my courses on scientific writing asked:

> How do I handle the situation when the supervisor is writing the manuscript?

The answer is simple. You yourself write the first draft before the supervisor calls for a writing session, as the following graduate student probably did (Ullrika Sahlin, 2010):

> In all papers . . . I produced the first draft of each manuscript and finished the writing in cooperation with the co-authors.

11
Popularized summary

Popularized summary is not used in all universities.

A thesis has three levels of language. The individual papers are written for the specialist, the overview for the non-specialist, and the popularized summary for the layperson. How do you find the level of the layperson? You may imagine a 12-year-old standing behind you, looking over your shoulder while you are writing.

When reading your popularized summary, the layperson first of all wants to know why you were captivated by the subject to such an extent that you were willing to spend four to six of the best years of your life studying it. Of course, what you did and what you found should be presented – but only briefly; this is not the place for lengthy details about your research. The layperson is also interested in the practical applications, i.e. in how treatment of diseases in human beings could benefit from your rat data.

Add elementary illustrations that you yourself may draw, so simple that they might qualify for a place in a children's book. If you think, "If I do that no one will take me seriously," then let me tell you that when Peter Englund, Secretary of the Swedish Academy that awards the Nobel Prize for Literature, was writing his thesis, his supervisor said that it was too easily understood: "You will not be taken seriously" (Chukri, 2008).

12

Acknowledgments

Intensifiers are said to weaken. Consider this:

> Special thanks to; [name] for valuable suggestions and skilful reflections concerning my research, [name] for fruitful discussions, [name] for excellent work, [name] for excellent help, [name] for excellent advice, [name] for helpful comments, [name] for fruitful discussions

Instead, try to be specific, as in this example (Rikard Nelander, 2009):

> First, I would like to thank my supervisor [name] for introducing me to the field of transport and optics in nanostructures and for always having his door open for questions and discussions. . . . I also would like to thank; . . . [name] for introducing me to solid-state physics, and [name] for leading me towards theoretical semiconductor physics. . . . [name] for the many discussions about quantum cascade lasers and semiconductor optics . . .
>
> A warm thank you goes to [name], with whom I have had the pleasure to share an office during most of my PhD studies. His refusal to learn Swedish during his four-year stay has taught me Danish . . .

or, like this, about quick revisions (Cristina Book, 2009):

> I want to express my gratitude to [name], for your thorough reviews of the text in all the papers (within 24 hours).

If you suffer from writer's block, the following could be a way out; only the two names have been deleted:

Thanks to:

My supervisor [name]
My co-supervisor [name]
My colleagues at the Gastroenterology Lab
My co-authors
Black Sabbath [a heavy metal band; I had to Google the name]
My friends
My family
Anna
Siri

The order in which those acknowledged are arranged is up to you to decide. However, the usual order is from the supervisor down to minor associates and up again to the family. If people whom you want to thank are not familiar with English, acknowledge them in their native language.

Writer's block was apparently not present in the following example.

Acknowledgments

I love this part of the thesis. I always read acknowledgments from other people's theses and really plan to have a wonderful time writing my own. So, where to begin . . .

Figure 12.1 shows the author of the above acknowledgments and illustrates the situation in which a female PhD candidate may have to live.

Figure 12.1 Before Children: I was thankful for the opportunity to obtain a university education and have a higher quality of life than my ancestors did. **After Children:** I am thankful to finish a complete thought without being interrupted. (Reproduced with permission from Mare Lõhmus, 2005.)

Grant-giving authorities

Those who have supported your studies financially should be acknowledged, even if you have already thanked them in your individual papers. But be careful how you present their names. If one of the names of the funding agencies is not in English, do *not* present the name in this manner:

> I am grateful for financial support from . . . Reumatikerförbundet

You should use either a translation alone or both a translation and the original name (Aladdin Mohammad, 2009):

> The studies presented in this thesis were supported by grants from . . .
> the Swedish Rheumatism Association (Reumatikerförbundet)

13

General introduction

Also called Background or just Introductory chapter. Some universities use an Introduction followed by a Review of the Literature. Consult the guidelines of your university to see what they recommend.

The general introduction is often far too long; occasionally up to 100 printed pages. About 10 printed pages may be sufficient. Brevity is a basic rule of scientific writing. Therefore, your general introduction should not include all papers that touched on your subject, but only those that could contribute to solving your problem. Try to avoid the usual platitudes in the opening sentences.

Openings

Avoid platitudes:

> Over the past century, scientific research has been very successful in understanding fundamental processes and in improving human living conditions but there are still many challenges ahead.

This could open any introduction, whatever the subject. Could you guess what it comes from? The answer is the Institute of Analytical Chemistry.

... and avoid general statements:

> We are facing perhaps the greatest challenge in the history of mankind – the shift from a depleting to a sustainable society. Politicians, industry, the scientific community and last but not least the people, together have a responsibility in making this happen. It will not be easy, but our future may depend on our success.

This is from an introduction of a thesis in biotechnology. Who could have guessed that?

Also, avoid empty words; note that four references are used to support what is obvious:

> Heart failure is a common condition that often leads to hospitalization.[1–4]

Instead, be specific, like this (Emeli Adell, 2009):

> The estimated number of road traffic fatalities worldwide is about 1.2 million each year. The number of injured could be as high as 50 million (Peden *et al.*, 2004).

Stating an astonishing fact can also be an effective opening (K. Markus Roupé, 2009):

> The skin is the largest organ of the human body ...

You can also omit needless information to get to the point, like this:

> ~~Stroke is the most common disorder in the group diseases referred to as cerebro-vascular diseases.~~ Stroke may be ischemic, meaning an infarct in the brain, or hemorrhagic, which implies an accumulation of blood in the skull vault.

The introduction is not the place to tell the story of how you were attracted to the subject. If you do want to relate that, do it in a *foreword*, placed first in your thesis. Below is a fine example in which a medical student coming home one day from his hospital duties found his pregnant wife with swollen face, hands, and feet, and with an alarmingly high blood pressure, indicating a condition that could lead to convulsion and coma. She was immediately admitted to hospital. The foreword continues:

> At that time I knew little about disorders in pregnancy, so right after we got the diagnosis I ran to the nearest book shop and bought my first book on hypertension in pregnancy.

Eventually, a healthy girl was born. Years later, her father defended a thesis with the title *Hypertension in Pregnancy. Effects of Calcium Channel Blockade* (Dag Wide-Swensson, 1994).

To include illustrations in the general introduction is recommended. You can reprint from textbooks or other articles (with permission) or from web domains (see Chapter 18, "Copyright"), or you can have them made. Also useful for catching the readers' interest could be to show a portrait of the person who has given his or her name to the disease being studied or the inventor of the main apparatus or method used.

14

Aims

Also called *Research questions*, *Objectives*, *Purpose* or *Scope* of the thesis.

Do not use abbreviations here; but if you do, explain them (see Chapter 8, "Abbreviations").

One concise sentence for each aim is often sufficient. You may present them as bullet points (as here) or in a paragraph of text. Instead of beginning these sentences with synonyms:

The aims were:
- to study ...
- to investigate ...
- to determine ...
- to examine ...
- to document ...

... try, as an umbrella, one of them, and avoid introducing synonyms (Alexey Schramko 2010):

The goals were to determine
- the effects of a single dose ...
- the mechanisms of ...
- the hemodynamic profile ...

Aims can also appear as questions (Rahmat Nadaffi, 2007):

- Why is an invasive species more successful in some areas than others? (Paper I)
- How do zebra mussels affect phytoplankton community structure in lakes? (Paper II)
- . . .

. . . or as hypothesis testing (Markus Andersson, 2005):

- Some red algae possess xanthophyll cycles (Papers I and II)
- Xanthophyll cycles in red algae are not strictly light-dependent (Paper III)
- . . .

15

Methods

Although this chapter is not included in the thesis of the sandwich format, the last pages on how to make use of photographs could be useful in your future writing.

Patients, subjects, or material

If you have one common group of subjects or samples, use a flow chart to show how they were allocated among the different studies. If you have two groups, create two flow charts. In Figure 15.1, three of four papers shared the same subjects.

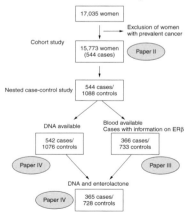

Figure 15.1 Study population for Papers II—IV. (Emily Sonestedt, 2008, with permission.)

Circles can be used in a similar manner, with circle size corresponding to the number of subjects; overlapping circles indicating that some studies had some features in common.

If each of your studies was based on different subjects or samples, use a table for the presentation.

Table 15.1 Clinical data from the five papers of the thesis.

Characteristics	Paper				
	I	II	III	IV	V
Number of patients	128	213	27	24	227
Number of tumors	128	213	35	56	238
Men : women	1 : 1.2	1 : 1.3	1 : 1.1	1.7 : 1	1 : 1.1
Mean age (range)	50 (20–84)	–[a]	49 (27–78)	49 (23–78)	71 (39–92)
MSI-high (%)[b]	46	44	66	96	23

[a] Not relevant for the study.
[b] MSI denotes Microsatellite instability.
Source: Adapted from Britta Halvarsson, 2007, with permission.

An overview of the study design could also help the reader, especially if the design varies from one study to the other; in the following example, three of the four studies have a different design.

Table 15.2 Design and participants

	Design	Participants (*n*)
Paper I	Qualitative interview study	19 parents (10 mothers and 9 fathers)
Paper II	Quantitative case-control study using questionnaires	22 parents with 66 matched controls
Paper III	Quantitative comparative study using questionnaires	66 parents with an abnormal finding (AF) in their fetus compared to a group of 1983 parents with normal findings (NF) in their foetus
Paper IV	Qualitative interview study	16 parents (9 mothers and 7 fathers)

Source: Adapted from Anna-Karin Larsson, 2009, with permission.

Methods

Having already described in detail the methods in the research papers, you may present this section on a non-specialist level in the overview. Choose words similar to those you would use in discussing the methods over lunch with a colleague from a specialty other than your own. Try to summarize the methods, as shown in Figure 15.2.

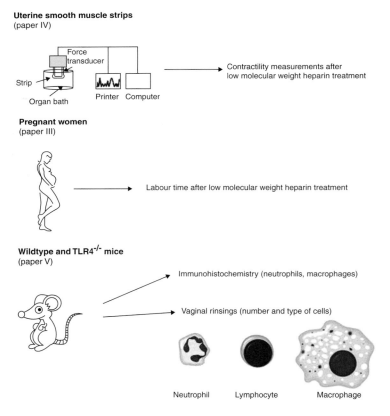

Figure 15.2 Shown here is part of a list of five methods used, presented with a touch of humor. (Anna Åkerud, 2009, with permission.)

A photo has the virtue of providing readers with a realistic view. The difficulty of seeing details in a photo can be solved by means of an explanatory drawing. However, the drawing must exactly depict the content of the photo and also be oriented in exactly the same direction, as shown in the example in Figure 15.3.

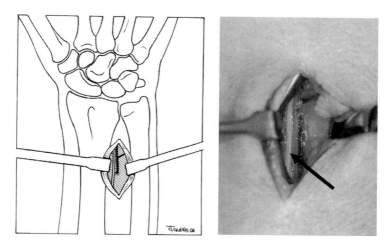

Figure 15.3 A drawing supporting a photo taken during surgery. (Niels O. B. Thomsen, 2009, with permission.)

Figure 15.4 shows a sketch supporting a microphotograph.

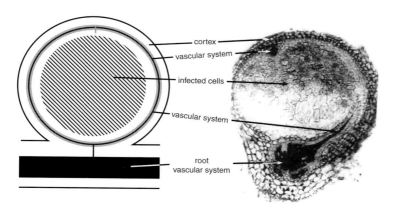

Figure 15.4 A scheme of a nodule of *L. japonicus* (left) with a microphotograph of such a nodule (right) with arrows pointing at the major morphological features. (Anna Maria Zdyb, 2008, with permission.)

In the following photo, the connections of the tubes are difficult to discern because it is taken against the light. (What you can clearly see, however, is that the photo was taken 17 minutes and 14 seconds past 10.) The photo cries out for a supporting drawing. Actually, a drawing could replace the photo.

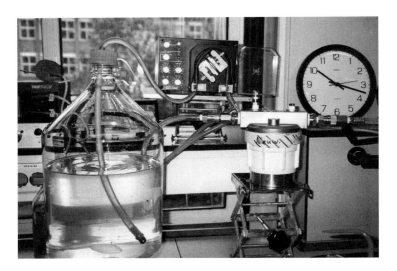

Figure 15.5 In Paper III large water samples of 200–500 L were filtered at the point of sampling [at the river] while small volume water samples, 10 L, were filtered in the laboratory as shown in the picture. (Reproduced from a thesis published in 2004, with permission.)

This photo was taken by the graduate student herself, she has told me. However, if you really want a photo, ask a professional photographer to take it. It may cost a lot, but you write a thesis only once in your life.

16
Results

This chapter is not included in the thesis of the sandwich format, but it contains tips on how to make illustrations and to write figure legends which can be useful when you write papers in the future.

Begin by referring specialist readers to the individual papers (Tapio Kurki, 1992).

> The detailed results are presented in the original communications, and therefore they are only briefly summarized here.

Then, in the overview, try to synthesize data from more than one paper. For example, one overview presented the results of all four individual papers in one single page; we can call it *Results at a glance* (Carin Staland Nyman, 2008). Another one summarized the findings of Papers III and IV in one illustrative drawing (Daniel Bexell, 2008). After such summaries, only the main points need to be highlighted. This approach may be better than a tedious repetition of the results paper by paper.

Data from the studies are often assembled in figures made especially for the overview and have thus passed no editorial scrutiny. Some representative figures will be scrutinized here. If the figure has a message, and most figures do, the message should be conveyed in the legend.

Circle diagram (also called *pie chart*)

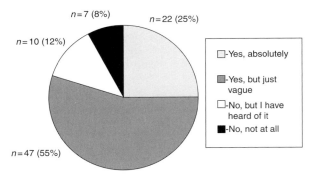

Figure 16.1 *[The author's own words are kept in each legend of the original figures in this chapter.]* Knowledge of IBS. Question 1: "Do you consider that you have knowledge about IBS?" (Reproduced from a thesis published in 2008, with permission.)

A separate key (in the box) forces the reader to go back and forth between the figure and the key to see what the segments represent (Figure 16.1). Label the segments directly (Figure 16.2). A good circle diagram starts with the largest segment at 12 o'clock and continues with proportionally smaller portions in the clockwise direction. The legend of the original Figure (16.1) does not convey the message, and IBS is undefined (IBS stands for *irritable bowel syndrome*). See the redrawn diagram (Figure 16.2) and its legend.

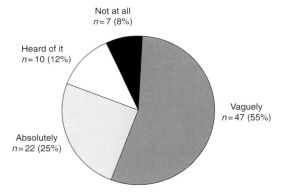

Figure 16.2 Redrawn version of Figure 16.1 and a rewritten legend including the main message:
Answers to a questionnaire on the knowledge of irritable bowel syndrome, completed by patients with this disease. Only 25% of the patients answered that they "absolutely" had knowledge of this syndrome.

Line graph

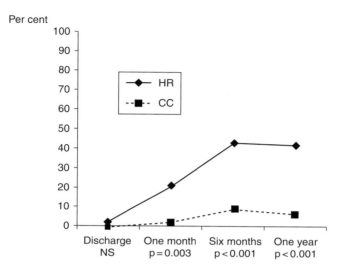

Figure 16.3 Proportions (percent) of participants reporting a full score (130) of the FES(S). (Reproduced from a thesis published in 2008, with permission.)

The two curves (Figure 16.3) need *not* be distinguished by both different kinds of lines and different data point symbols. A solid line alone will suffice (Figure 16.4). The horizontal axis (Figure 16.3) is misleadingly contracted because the distance between the first two tick marks represents one month, whereas the same distance between the following ticks represents several months. This problem can be solved by altering the time scale (Figure 16.4). The key needs a key of its own. HR denotes home rehabilitation; CC, conventional care. And FES(S) stands for Falls Efficacy Scale (Swedish version). Note that a full label to the vertical axis is placed parallel to the axis.

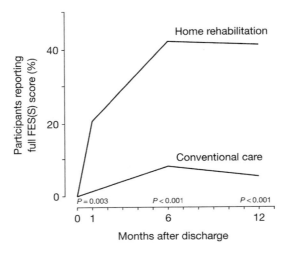

Figure 16.4 Alternative display of Figure 16.3 and a revised version of its legend: Various daily activities were significantly better performed in home rehabilitation than in conventional care. FES(S) denotes Falls Efficacy Scale (Swedish version).

Column chart (also called *bar chart*)

All columns in Figure 16.5 may be shown in the same gray tone (Figure 16.6). The columns are cropped, and you normally have to indicate that fact by cutting off each column as well as the vertical axis (Figure 16.6).

However, in this case, the columns seem to be better shown at their full length (Figure 16.7). Concerning the legend: your own results should be presented in the past tense; thus *lowered*, not *lower*. The details of the statistics should appear in the methods section.

It is, however, redundant to indicate a mean value by means of a column (Figures 16.5, 16.6 and 16.7). In Figure 16.8, the mean values are marked by a data point symbol (□); note also the exact *P*-values.

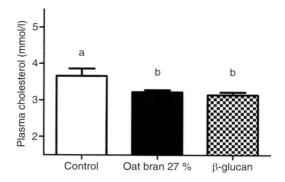

Figure 16.5 Isolated beta-glucans lower plasma cholesterol to the same level as oat bran in the C57BL/6 mice fed an atherogenic diet. N=10 [in each group], statistics performed with ANOVA followed by Tukey's multiple comparison test. Bars with different letters differ significantly, p<0.05. (Reproduced from a thesis published in 2009, with permission.)

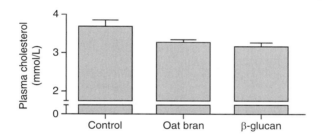

Figure 16.6 Alternative display of Figure 16.5.

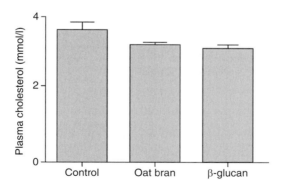

Figure 16.7 Another, alternative display of Figure 16.5 and a rewritten legend: Pure β-glucans lowered plasma cholesterol to the same level as that of oat bran; both values were significantly reduced compared to the control ($P < 0.05$). Oat bran concentration 27%. Mean values and SEM (standard error of the mean) for 10 observations in each group.

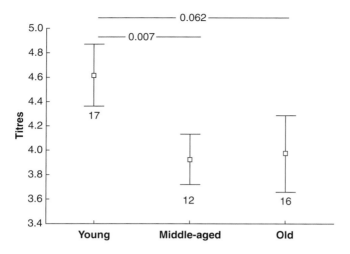

Figure 16.8 The immune response of female flycatchers to sheep red blood cells. *Young age* denotes 1-year-old; *middle-aged*, 3-year-old; and *old*, 5 to 6-year-old. Numbers below error bars indicate sample size. Mean values and SEM. (Adapted from Joanna Sendecka, 2007, with permission.)

A message could be added to the legend as a second sentence:

> Young individuals had a higher immune response than did older ones.

Box-plot

The *box-and-whisker plot* (*box-plot*) has become a popular form of presenting data. Computer programs have standardized the use of it – for example, the band in the middle of the box is always the *median*, which is the correct term to use in most results in biomedical science. Figure 16.9 is a fine example; although appearing in the overview of the thesis (Anna Åkerud, 2009), this figure had also been included in one of the individual papers and thus has passed editorial scrutiny.

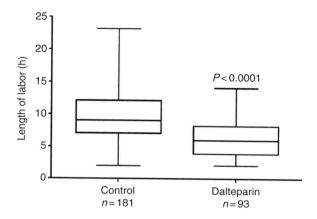

Figure 16.9 The effect of dalteparin on duration of labor in women delivered vaginally compared to that of controls matched according to age and parity. (Reprinted by permission from Informa Healthcare: *Acta Obstet Gynecol Scand* 2010;89(1):147–50, Ekman-Ordeberg G, Åkerud A, Dubicke A, *et al.* Does Low Molecular Weight Heparin shorten Term Labor? Copyright © 2010.)

Again, a message could be added to the legend as a second sentence:

Dalteparin shortened labor.

3D graph

Most computer programs easily display the three-dimensional graph. As a result, this type of graph is seen more and more often in published reports. Unfortunately, the ease with which it can be created often leads to its use even in cases where the data have only two dimensions. A third dimension is thus falsely introduced. A true third dimension is extremely uncommon in research work. Figure 16.10 shows an example of this rare species.

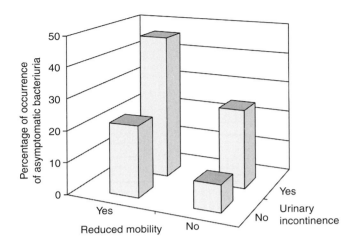

Figure 16.10 Estimated occurrence of asymptomatic bacteriuria in women related to urinary incontinence and reduced mobility. (Adapted from Nils Rodhe, 2008, with permission.)

In this case, a message could replace the whole text of the legend:

> Asymptomatic bacteriuria occurred more often in women with both reduced mobility and urinary incontinence than in those without these conditions

Note that a purely *descriptive* figure, for example, the method used, probably has no message to provide, as in this (which actually belongs in the methods section) (Maria Bernsand, 2006):

> Schematic picture showing a rat with a microdialysis probe in position

Color illustration

Color illustrations are said to enhance a presentation, but they must add something and not just be decorative. If you include color photos, such as histological micrographs, in your individual papers, less-expensive black-and-white photos will suffice in the thesis overview. However, you may not find it necessary to reproduce them there at all, as the non-specialist reader usually finds these difficult to interpret.

Color drawing and graphs may be used, but remember that about 10% of males and 1% of females suffer from color blindness and are unable to distinguish between red and green, which both appear brown. For example, when you are comparing two lines in a graph, it is best to use red and blue.

17

General discussion

You open your general discussion in either of two manners: (a) by answering the questions or suggestions put forward in the aims, or (b) by discussing the methodology – the latter because one of the goals of a thesis is to learn how to use scientific methods and to get to know their limitations, not primarily to make discoveries.

Which of these you choose depends on the purpose, the direction, and the results of your research. We begin with the first alternative.

General discussion

Discussion of the results

Open this section by explaining how you achieved your aims. In one thesis (Anders Bergström, 1994), two of the aims were to determine:

- a technique for subretinal transplantation of retinal cells
- the survival ... of donor cells

... and the discussion of the results began with subheadings for each aim:

Transplantation procedure
The subretinal transplantation technique that we have developed has turned out to be easy and [has given] good and consistent results.

Transplant cell survival
The survival rate was ...

What makes the writing of these sentences especially good is that the author used almost exactly the same wording as in the sentences describing the aims. Here is no place for synonyms. The readers must know for certain what you mean. Remember that more than half the scientists worldwide have English as a second language, and such readers may become uncertain if you use synonyms.

Then consider the whole picture in a general discussion of the results. Methodology considerations follow thereafter. However, if you have chosen to begin the discussion with the second alternative, you may start as follows.

General discussion

Methodological considerations

Present the strengths and weaknesses of your individual papers, such as opinions of any shortcomings in study design, limitations in methods, flaws in analysis, or in validity of assumptions. I have picked up a few subtitles from two theses, so you can see what could be included, for example, this (Margaretha Danerek, 2010):

Trustworthy
Validity
Reliability

or this (Hanne Kristine Hegaard, 2009):

> Selection bias
> Information bias
> Confounding

Discussion of results thereafter follows. The rest of the discussion has a layout similar to that in the individual papers, as shown in the following.

Comparison with other studies

Contrary to the case in the general introduction, where you have discussed *all* relevant works, here in the general discussion you should discuss *only* those findings by others that you can directly connect to your results. Beginning with your most significant observation, you start the comparison with studies whose results are largely consistent with your own. Then consider studies less compatible with yours. Conclude with any results that contradict your findings. Thereafter continue with the next most important observation, and so on. All along the way, discuss similarities and differences. If you cannot explain conflicting evidence, you could suggest how the discrepancy might be resolved by a new trial.

Conclusions

What you are to include here is exactly what you already should have written in the figure legends or the table titles – the message. Thus, instead of waiting to do the hard work until you reach the conclusion section, do it directly when you write the legends. Then you just have to gather what you have already written.

Implications for further research

Beginners often overshoot their mark and speculate too much, which is negatively noted in reviewers' comments, like this one concerning an individual paper:

> The experimental outcome is certainly unexpected and extremely interesting, and the experiments were performed well. But the authors need to be more cautious in drawing unwarranted conclusions [and implications].

Reasonable speculations may be made, for example, from observations under way from your next work.

18

Copyright

Although all illustrations in a thesis should have a credit line, pictures without such a line are found far too often. Even with a credit line, the text is often incomplete and even incorrect. For example, if you are to reproduce a figure from another publication, you must obtain permission from both the publisher and the author and then credit the source at the end of your figure legend. The following credit line, i.e. "*288*," is inappropriate:

> Figure 4.5 [figure legend] (288)

The figure *288* refers to the reference list of the overview where we find an article published by *Nature*. I emailed the publisher of *Nature* and asked for a credit line for this particular figure. They sent me this:

> Reprinted by permission from Macmillan Publishers Ltd: *Nature* 402, 377–385 (25 November 1999) doi:10.1038/46483, Lancaster *et al.*, Structure of fumarate reductase from *Wolinella succinogenes* at 2.2 Å resolution. Copyright © 2009. All rights reserved.

This text from Macmillan should have been used as a credit line, instead of reference figure *288*.

If you have taken two or more illustrations from the same source, you should repeat the credit line under each figure. If the publisher requires a credit line as lengthy as that of *Nature* above, the line could be included in the legend of the first figure and the others would say this:

> (Permission as in Figure 1.)

If, however, the publisher and author allow you to use a shorter form, this could be repeated under each figure, as below (Margareta Claesson, 2008):

> Figure 2 [figure legend] (Hogan *et al.* 1971, reproduced with permission.)
> Figure 3 [figure legend] (Hogan *et al.* 1971, reproduced with permission.)

Illustrators occasionally receive thanks in the acknowledgments – if thanked at all. If you give them a credit line in the figure legend, the artists will love it (Ingrid Berkestedt, 2009):

> Figure 2 [figure legend] (Illustration by [name].)

In a similar manner, you yourself could be credited (Margareta Claesson, 2008):

> Figure 1 [figure legend] (Author's picture.)

or (the same credit line reformulated):

> Figure 1 [figure legend] (Photograph taken by me)

If you use pictures provided by a person not involved in your research, acknowledge this person (Nedim Selimovic, 2009):

> Figure 1 [figure legend] (Courtesy of [name] MD, Dept. of Pathology, Sahlgrenska University Hospital.)

If you include figures from your individual papers, you must state which picture from which paper you have reprinted in the overview (Magnus Carlquist, 2008):

> Figure 14 [figure legend] (Figure 6d in Paper VI.)

You should also have permission from the publisher to reproduce this figure and add a credit line to the figure legend (see the last paragraph of the fictitious permission letter on the first page of Chapter 9, "List of publications").

Online images

Reproducing online images that are available for free use can be tricky. The following text is from one of the initial pages of a thesis published in 2008:

> Cover image:
> Cyclooxygenase-I with bound ibuprofen
> From *Wikimedia commons.*
> Used with permission (public domain)

This wording may confuse the reader, as the picture can be used without permission; actually you cannot obtain permission even if you want to. The reader is probably better served by this:

> From *Wikimedia commons* (public domain)
> Use allowed without formal permission

The last sentence could be removed, as in Figure 18.1 (Di Wang, 2009).

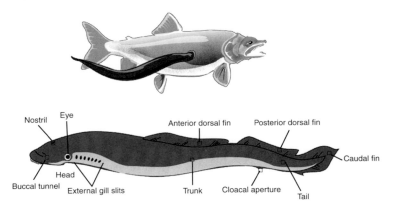

Figure 18.1 Top: The lamprey feeds on fish by attaching with its suction mouth. Bottom: Illustration of the general anatomy of the lamprey. (Public domain image from *Wikimedia Commons*.)

(This picture I took directly from *Wikimedia Commons* without asking anyone. The illustrator, Mariana Ruiz Villarreal, had agreed to place it in the public domain.)

Creative Commons License

Although images are still (December 2011) uploaded to the public domain to be used for free (like those above), more and more people chose to put their uploaded pictures under the *Creative Commons License*. That means that the creator of a picture sets the terms under which the picture may be used. These terms are given at the web page in which the picture appears. At the minimum, you should attribute the creator and do so even if you alter the picture. Those were the restrictions for the use of the drawing below (Figure 18.2). I have suggested a credit line.

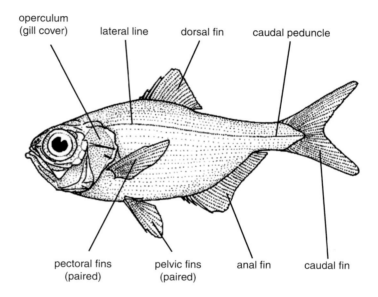

Figure 18.2 Anatomy of *Beryx splendens* (*Splendid Alfonso*). (Reproduced from *Wikimedia Commons*; drawing by Dr Tony Ayling.)

Photo of a human being

If you want to publish a photo of a human being, you must obtain written permission. An example of an agreement letter to be signed by the person depicted is shown in Figure 18.4. To protect the individual's anonymity, a black band across the eyes does not prevent the patient from being identified any more than dark glasses do. A better manner is to properly crop the photo, as shown in Figure 18.3 (taken from a Case Report).

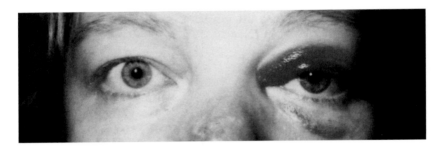

Figure 18.3 Lesions of the eyelids of the left side. The author has solved the problem of concealing the patient's identity by cropping the photo. You cannot even see if the person is a man or woman. It is a woman. (Reproduced, with permission, from E. Tóth, U. Havelius and F. T. Fork (1998). Orbital hemorrhage as a complication of gastroscopy. *Endoscopy* 1998;30(8):S89.)

Even a naked individual can be ensured anonymity, if the person is shown in silhouette (see Chapter 3, "Front cover illustration," Figure 3.1).

If you show a photo of a child, you should state in the figure legend that you have the consent of the parents. The following statement concerns a photo of a newborn (Fredrik Ahlsson, 2008):

> Figure 6 [figure legend] (Consent for publication was obtained from the parents.)

No credit line needed

As mentioned at the beginning of this section, all figures in the thesis overview should have a credit line. The following note on one of the initial pages could be regarded as an exception to this rule (Charlotta Borell Lövstedt, 2008):

> All photos are taken by [me] if not otherwise stated

Obtaining permission

Most publishers of scientific journals provide online forms for requesting permission to reproduce pictures. (For images online you have other directions to follow, as outlined above.) Concerning the request to the author, your permission letter should include the text you would like to use and, if you have modified the illustration, also the adapted figure. You may use a template (Figure 18.5) that you can save on your computer. I always suggest as a model a short credit line when I seek permission; sometimes the publisher and author allow me to use it.

Copyright infringement

What happens to people who are discovered to have violated copyright? First-time transgressors, I have been told, will only receive a letter from the publisher that will ask them to seek permission afterwards. But the infringement has another aspect — the principle of ethics. Actually, as you are aiming at the highest academic degree, people expect you to do things right. You are seen as a model for those coming after you. So seek permissions for anything borrowed and make an effort to formulate the credit lines correctly.

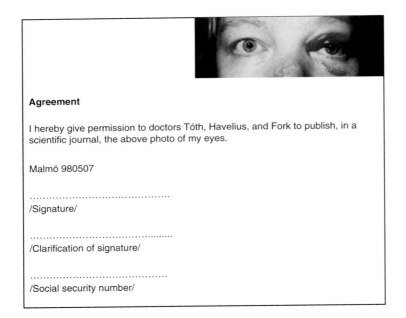

Agreement

I hereby give permission to doctors Tóth, Havelius, and Fork to publish, in a scientific journal, the above photo of my eyes.

Malmö 980507

....
/Signature/

....
/Clarification of signature/

....
/Social security number/

Figure 18.4 A letter requesting permission to use a photo. [Translated from Swedish.] In this case, the photo was pasted onto a sheet of paper that already had the text written down, and the montage was then copied on a color photocopier so that photo and text were integrated on one sheet of paper. (Adapted from Tóth, Havelius and Fork, 1998, with permission.)

16 Oct 2011

Ulf Havelius, MD, PhD
Dept of Ophthalmology
Malmö University Hospital
University of Lund
Malmö
Sweden

Dear Dr Havelius,

I am writing a book on compilation theses with the working title, How to Prepare a Scientific Doctoral Dissertation Based on Research Papers, to be published by Cambridge University Press.

I would greatly appreciate your permission to reproduce figure 1 from:

E. Tóth, U. Havelius, ET Fork. Orbital hemorrhage as a complication of gastroscopy. Endoscopy 1998;30:S89.

and the letter of permission from the patient. I have also enclosed the text I want to use.

Acknowledgments of the source will be printed on the page where the figure appears, as follows:

Reproduced from Tóth, Havelius and Fork, 1998, with permission.

A full reference will be given in the reference list. If this form of acknowledgement is not sufficient, please indicate how the credit line should appear.

Many thanks for your help.

Yours sincerely,

Björn Gustavii, MD, PhD
Clemenstorget 3
SE-222 21 Lund, Sweden
bjorngustavii@telia.com

Figure 18.5 A template to be used when requesting, by email, permission to use copyrighted material. (Reproduced with permission from Tóth, Havelius and Fork, 1998.)

19

A dissertation worth considering

I will show you a dissertation with a layout that may be worth considering. Some aspects of the presentation are in line with those emphasized in this book. That is a dissertation (by Christopher James Clark, published 2009) at the University of California, Berkeley. Excerpts are presented on the following pages, with comments.

At the time the dissertation was filed, that is, submitted to the Graduate Division at Berkeley, two chapters were published as articles, the third was in revision by the author, and the fourth had been submitted for publication.

Sorry to say, the author was not allowed to orally defend his dissertation, because Berkeley seems to be unique in having no dissertation defense. Actually, for papers still *in manuscript*, an author could benefit from feedback during a defense process when making the final revisions of the articles before submission for publication.

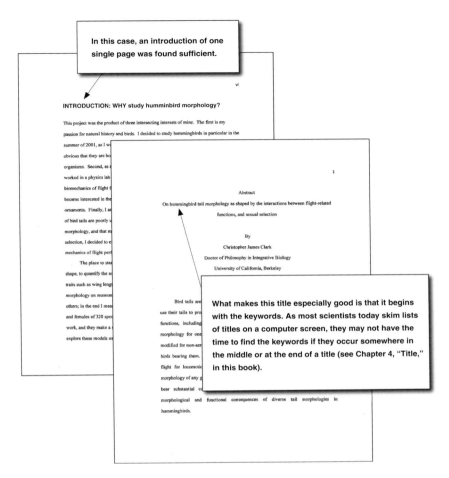

Figure 19.1 One can argue against the rationale of a long introduction that repeats what is already said in the four individual papers' introductory chapters. A short introduction presenting the theme of the thesis may be sufficient. (Christopher James Clark, 2009, with permission.)

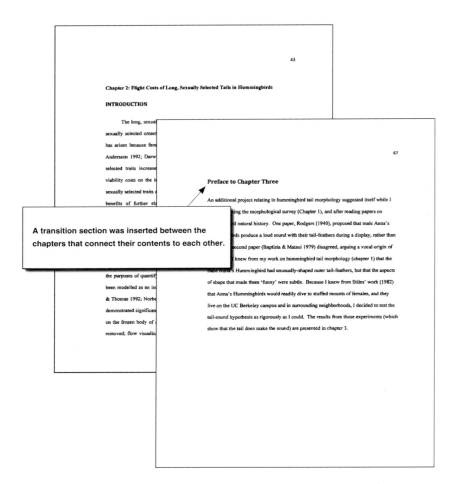

Figure 19.2 The transitional sections between the chapters serve as a common thread linking the various parts into a coherent unit. Such sections are common in US, as well as Australian, theses. I found this highly recommendable. (Christopher James Clark, 2009, with permission.)

In the published article, this title had a subtitle added by the editor of the journal that highlighted the novelty of the study: *The Anna's hummingbird chirps with its tail: a new mechanism of sonation in birds.* The author had preferred the original title (see below), not the above title introduced by the journal, he has told me, but, nevertheless, the new title is more informative for the non-specialist.

Chapter 3: The Anna's Hummingbird Chirps With Its Tail

INTRODUCTION

Acoustic communication plays an important role in bird behavior, sexual selection (Kroodsma & Byers 1991), and speciation (Price 1998). While the mechanisms of bird vocalizations have received considerable attention (Fletcher & Tarnopolsky 1999; Greenewalt 1968; Suthers et al. 1999), birds also produce a diversity of mechanical (non-vocal) sounds that are poorly described. Mechanical sounds are not created by the syrinx, but by other parts of the animal such as the wings or tail. They may be adventitious, produced incidentally and involuntarily as the part of some other behavior, or sonations

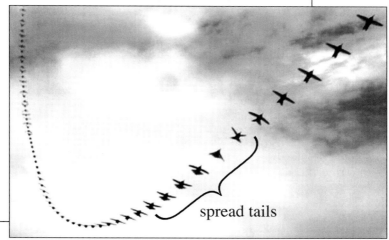

spread tails

Figure 1. A composite image of a male Anna's hummingbird diving to a female, created using high-speed video. Consecutive image are 0.01 s apart. During the dive, males spread their tails for 0.06 s (n=5 videos) and simultaneously produce a loud sound (element C_{dive} in figure 2a) for 0.05 s (n=53 sound recordings). Videos of two dives are available in the electronic supplementary material.

Figure 19.3 A fine illustration with a legend that explains not only what the figure shows but also what it is meant to say. Very good! (Reprinted by permission from the Royal Society: *Proc Biol Sci* 2008 April 22;275(1637):955–62, Clark CJ, Feo TJ, The Anna's hummingbird chirps with its tail: a new mechanism of sonation in birds.)

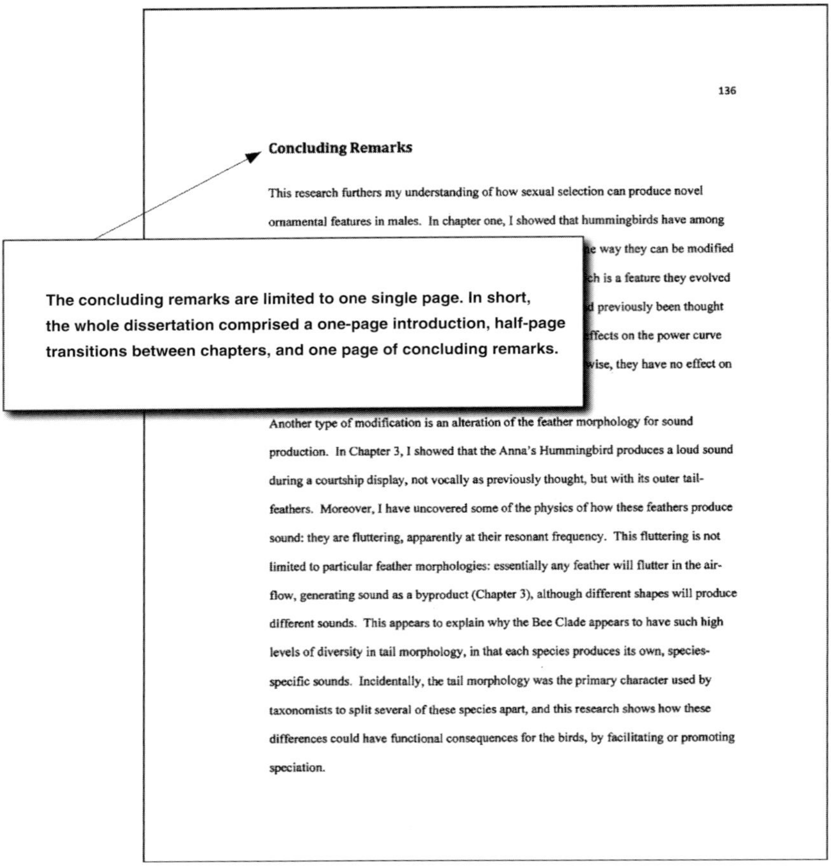

136

Concluding Remarks

This research furthers my understanding of how sexual selection can produce novel ornamental features in males. In chapter one, I showed that hummingbirds have among

...e way they can be modified

...h is a feature they evolved

...d previously been thought

...ffects on the power curve

...wise, they have no effect on

Another type of modification is an alteration of the feather morphology for sound production. In Chapter 3, I showed that the Anna's Hummingbird produces a loud sound during a courtship display, not vocally as previously thought, but with its outer tail-feathers. Moreover, I have uncovered some of the physics of how these feathers produce sound: they are fluttering, apparently at their resonant frequency. This fluttering is not limited to particular feather morphologies: essentially any feather will flutter in the air-flow, generating sound as a byproduct (Chapter 3), although different shapes will produce different sounds. This appears to explain why the Bee Clade appears to have such high levels of diversity in tail morphology, in that each species produces its own, species-specific sounds. Incidentally, the tail morphology was the primary character used by taxonomists to split several of these species apart, and this research shows how these differences could have functional consequences for the birds, by facilitating or promoting speciation.

The concluding remarks are limited to one single page. In short, the whole dissertation comprised a one-page introduction, half-page transitions between chapters, and one page of concluding remarks.

Figure 19.4 Similar points as in the introductory section could be made for the short concluding remarks: do you really need a comprehensive general discussion when each of the individual papers has its own discussion? Probably not. (Christopher James Clark, 2009, with permission.)

Appendix A
To the authorities at the graduate division

This appendix is written for those universities that do not yet allow article-based theses but are contemplating introducing them. If you decide on this alternative format, the discussion below may give you hints on what to add to the doctoral guidelines of your university.

Article-based theses vs. traditional monographs

In the *article-based thesis*, the accepted papers have "been scrutinized by international peer review, probably more prestigious than local committees" (Carlino, 2006). The article-based thesis gives students the opportunity to begin publishing early in their academic careers. One candidate put it this way: "You can graduate with a degree and a publication record. This is a wonderful kick-start to an academic career" (Kumpulainen, 2008). After all, one goal of a university is to produce scientific papers publishable in refereed journals.

After graduating with a *traditional monograph*, the graduates can be stricken with "Post-Dissertation Burnout," meaning that few journal publications will eventually grow out of their thesis. Important research findings may therefore languish on the shelves of libraries. That does not happen after graduation with an article-based thesis, because most or all of its papers are already published, are *in press*, or have been submitted. Candidates who publish throughout their candidacy receive ongoing peer review, improving their writing skills.

Guidelines ahead of their time

I looked into the online guidelines for doctoral dissertations of the top 50 US universities and the top 10 Australian universities and found that almost all of them accept article-based theses. Some of them also allow electronic reprints and preprints to be inserted as chapters. The conclusions below are based mainly upon these US and Australian guidelines.

Number and quality of papers required

Most institutions require a minimum of three papers. These papers should be accepted by or be publishable in peer-reviewed journals; some disciplines list the journals that are approved.

Status of papers

Some disciplines insist that all thesis articles be published as a requirement for graduation; others that they be presented in publishable format, ready to be submitted after the candidate's defense. The first option is problematic to the candidate, because of long publication timelines for some journals. As described by Duke and Beck (1999), it is not unusual to wait more than 6 months for the process of reviewing a manuscript submitted for publication, and then to wait again while the candidate revises the manuscript. And when the paper is finally ready to go to press, there may be another wait, often of 4–6 months. This option is not advisable.

The other model, that is, when no manuscript is submitted before graduation, has one advantage: the candidate could well benefit from feedback during a defense process before making the final revisions of the articles.

However, a middle-of-the-road approach may be recommendable, that is, at least one publication either accepted for publication or undergoing revision following review. Some disciplines adopt this course.

Publishing during enrollment only

Most universities stress that works done before enrollment in the doctoral program are not allowed to be included.

Authorship

The graduate student is usually placed first in the multi-author by-line. The candidate writes the first draft of a paper, which is then revised by the supervisor. Publishing with a supervisor enriches the candidate's experience of publication.

In multi-authored papers, the candidate must indicate which portions of the papers are his or her own work and which are the work of the co-authors. Some universities require a signed statement by contributing authors.

The future

In the hard sciences such as biology, medicine, and technology, the traditional monograph thesis seems to be slowly disappearing. The article-based thesis may also be becoming increasingly common in other disciplines as well – even, for example, in Drama and Art & Design.

Literature cited

Abhyankar, A. 2009. *Mitochondrial and chromosomal genomics in type 2 diabetes.* (Dissertation.) Lund, Sweden: University of Lund.

Adell, E. 2009. *Driver experience and acceptance of driver support systems – a case of speed adaptation.* (Dissertation.) Lund, Sweden: University of Lund.

Ahlsson, F. 2008. *Being born large for gestational age. Metabolic and epidemiological studies.* (Dissertation.) Uppsala, Sweden: Uppsala University.

Åkerud, A. 2009. *Uterine remodeling during pregnancy. Studies on the effect of heparin/heparan sulfate.* (Dissertation.) Lund, Sweden: University of Lund.

Andersson, M. 2005. *Pigment and acclimation patterns in marine red algae exposed to oxidative stress.* (Dissertation.) Uppsala, Sweden: Uppsala University.

Baranto, A. 2005. *Traumatic high-load injuries in the adolescent spine. Clinical, radiological and experimental studies.* (Dissertation.) Gothenburg, Sweden: The Sahlgrenska Academy of Gothenburg University.

Berglund, H. 2009. *The threat from non indigenous species. Ecosystem vulnerability, global distribution and co-occurrences with other major threats.* (Dissertation.) Lund, Sweden: University of Lund.

Bergström, A. 1994. *Experimental retinal cell transplants.* (Dissertation.) Lund, Sweden: University of Lund.

Berkestedt, I. 2009. *Host response in sepsis.* (Dissertation.) Lund, Sweden: University of Lund.

Bernsand, M. 2006. *Physiological and pathophysiological regulation of ECL cell activity.* (Dissertation.) Lund, Sweden: University of Lund.

Bexell, D. 2008. *Stem cell based therapy of malignant brain tumors. Mesenchymal and neural precursor cells as migratory vehicles in experimental gliomas.* (Dissertation.) Lund, Sweden: University of Lund.

Book, C. 2009, *Rheumatoid arthritis. Body composition, bone loss, and mortality.* (Dissertation.) Lund, Sweden: University of Lund.

Borell Lövstedt, C. 2008. *Hydrodynamics of very shallow lakes. A study in Lake Krankesjön, Sweden.* (Dissertation.) Lund, Sweden: University of Lund

Butt, S. 2011. *Reproductive factors and breast cancer. Parity, breastfeeding and genetic predisposition in relation to risk and prognosis.* (Dissertation.) Malmö, Sweden: Skåne University Hospital.

Carlino, P. 2006. EATAW (European Association for the Teaching of Academic Writing) email forum. www.eataw.org/listserv/ Reference 87, in the forum (accessed 9 December 2006).

Carlquist, M. 2008. *Enzymatic reduction of ketones.* (Dissertation.) Lund, Sweden: University of Lund.

Chukri, R. 2008. [Englund ignored the academic rules on how to write.] *Sydsvenskan [The South Swedish Daily News]*, August 24.

Claesson, M. 2008. *Corneal transplant outcome. A Swedish register.* (Dissertation.) Gothenburg, Sweden: The Sahlgrenska Academy of Gothenburg University.

Clark, C. J. 2009. *On hummingbird tail morphology as shaped by the interactions between flight-related functions, and sexual selection.* (Dissertation.) Berkeley, CA: University of California.

Danerek, M. 2010. *Decision-making in critical situations during pregnancy and birth.* (Dissertation.) Lund, Sweden: University of Lund.

Duke, N. K.; Beck, S. W. 1999. Education should consider alternative formats for dissertation. *Educational Researcher* **28**:31–9.

Ek, S. 1995. *Fetal hematopoietic cells in early gestation. Aspects in view of fetal transplantation.* (Dissertation.) Stockholm, Sweden: Karolinska Institutet.

Ekqvist, S. 2008. *Clinical and experimental studies of contact allergy to stent metals, with focus on gold.* (Dissertation.) Malmö, Sweden: Malmö University Hospital.

Hallberg, I. 2009. *Health-related quality of life in postmenopausal women with osteoporotic fractures.* (Dissertation.) Linköping, Sweden: Linköping University.

Halvarsson, B. 2007. *Morphological features and mismatch repair in colorectal tumors.* (Dissertation.) Lund, Sweden: University of Lund.

Hegaard, H. K. 2009. *Pregnancy and leisure time physical activity.* (Dissertation.) Lund, Sweden: University of Lund.

Henningsson, P. 2010. *Always on the wing. Fluid dynamics, flight performance and flight behavior of common swifts.* (Dissertation.) Lund, Sweden: University of Lund.

Holback, S. 2009. *Proteolytic processing of the Alzheimer APP protein family during neuronal differentiation.* (Dissertation.) Stockholm, Sweden: University of Stockholm.

Karim, F. 2009. *Genders matter. Understanding of access barriers to community-based tuberculosis care in Bangladesh.* (Dissertation.) Stockholm, Sweden: Karolinska Institutet.

Köbler, S. 2007. *Bilateral hearing aids for bilaterally hearing-impaired persons – always the best choice?* (Dissertation.) Stockholm, Sweden: Karolinska Institutet.

Kuendig, H. 2009. *Empty glasses and broken bones. Epidemiological studies on alcohol and injuries treated at an emergency department in Switzerland.* (Dissertation.) Stockholm, Sweden: Karolinska Institutet.

Kurki, T. 1992. *Preterm birth. A clinical, biochemical and bacteriological study.* (Dissertation.) Helsinki, Finland: University of Helsinki.

Kumpulainen, K. 2008. Google search: "Thesis by publication" cicero kumpulainen, strif.is/phd-supervision/files/2008/12/thesis_by_publication.pdf (accessed 7 July 2010).

Lahti, R. A. 2005. *From findings to statistics: an assessment of Finish medical cause-of-death information in relation to underlying-cause coding.* (Dissertation.) Helsinki, Finland: University of Helsinki.

Larsson, A. K. 2009. *Parents' experiences and reactions when an unexpected finding in their foetus is revealed at a routine ultrasound examination. A multi method study.* (Dissertation.) Lund, Sweden: University of Lund.

Lind, O. 2011. *Bird vision. Spatial acuity and colour discrimination in bright and dim light.* (Dissertation.) Lund, Sweden: University of Lund.

Lindström, D. 2008. *The impact of tobacco use on postoperative complications.* (Dissertation.) Stockholm, Sweden: Karolinska Institute.

Ljungberg, E. 2008. *Hand injuries in young children. Incidences, aetiologies, injury patterns and costs.* (Dissertation.) Malmö, Sweden: Malmö University Hospital.

Lõhmus, M. 2005, *Endocrinology, behaviour and immunity related to energetic condition in birds.* (Dissertation.) Gothenburg, Sweden: The Sahlgrenska Academy of Gothenburg University.

Mohammad, A. 2009. *Studies on the epidemiology and outcome of primary systemic vasculitis.* (Dissertation.) Lund, Sweden: University of Lund.

Nadaffi, R. 2007. *The invasion of the zebra mussel. Effects on phytoplankton community structure and ecosystem function.* (Dissertation.) Uppsala, Sweden: Uppsala University.

Nelander, R. 2009. *Lineshape in quantum cascade lasers. Temperature, screening and broadening.* (Dissertation.) Lund, Sweden: University of Lund.

Nilsson, M. H. 2009. *Balance performance in people with Parkinson's disease. Effects of subthalamic deep brain stimulation.* (Dissertation.) Lund, Sweden: University of Lund.

Osmancevic, A. 2009. *Vitamin D status in psoriasis patients treated with UVB therapy.* (Dissertation.) Uppsala, Sweden: Uppsala University.

Padmos, R. 2009. *Inflammatory monocytes in bipolar disorder and related endocrine autoimmune diseases.* (Dissertation.) Rotterdam, the Netherlands: Erasmus University Rotterdam.

Rodhe, N. 2008. *Asymptomatic bacteruria in the elderly.* (Dissertation.) Uppsala, Sweden: Uppsala University.

Roupé, K. M. 2009. *Epidermal reactions to injury with implications for innate immunity.* (Dissertation.) Lund, Sweden: University of Lund.

Sahlin, U. 2010. *From data to decision. Learning by probabilistic risk analysis of biological invasions.* (Dissertation.) Lund, Sweden: University of Lund.

Saunders, D. L. 2008. *Ecology and conservation of the swift parrot – an endangered austral migrant.* (Dissertation.) Canberra, Australia: Australian National University.

Schramko, A. 2010. *Postoperative volume therapy in cardiac surgery. Effects on hemostatic and circulatory variables.* (Dissertation.) Helsinki, Finland: University of Helsinki.

Selimovic, N. 2009. *Pulmonary hypertension. Clinical and pathophysiological studies.* (Dissertation.) Gothenburg, Sweden: The Sahlgrenska Academy of Gothenburg University.

Sendecka, J. 2007. *Age, longevity and life-history trade-offs in the collared flycatcher (Ficedula albicollis).* (Dissertation.) Uppsala, Sweden: Uppsala University.

Sonestedt, E. 2008. *Plant foods, plasma enterolactone and breast cancer with a focus on estrogen receptor status genetic variation.* (Dissertation.) Lund, Sweden: University of Lund.

Sorbring, E. 2005. *Girls' and boys' views of conflicts with parents.* (Dissertation.) Göteborg, Sweden: The Sahlgrenska Academy at Göteborg University.

Staland Nyman, C. 2008. *Domestic workload and multiple roles. Epidemiological findings on health and sickness absence in women.* (Dissertation.) Gothenburg, Sweden: The Sahlgrenska Academy of Gothenburg University.

Svedberg, L. 2009. *Cold feet in children with neurological disorders.* (Dissertation.) Lund, Sweden: University of Lund.

Tasevska-Dinevska, G. 2008. *Gender aspects on heart failure.* (Dissertation.) Malmö, Sweden: Malmö University Hospital.

Theander, E. 2005. *Living and dying with primary Sjögren's Syndrome. Studies on aetiology, treatment, lymphoma, survival and predictors.* (Dissertation.) Malmö, Sweden: University of Lund.

Thomsen, N. O. B. 2009. *Carpal tunnel syndrome and diabetes. Surgical outcome and nerve pathology.* (Dissertation.) Malmö, Sweden: Malmö University Hospital.

Torkzad, M. R. 2006. *Magnetic resonance imaging of rectum. Diagnostic and therapy related aspects.* (Dissertation.) Stockholm, Sweden: Karolinska Institutet.

Tóth, E.; Havelius, U.; Fork, F. T. 1998. Orbital hemorrhage as a complication of gastroscopy. *Endoscopy* **30**(8 Oct):S89.

Vinther, A. 2008. *Rib stress fractures in elite rowers.* (Dissertation.) Lund, Sweden: University of Lund.

Wang, D. 2009. *Ion channels and intrinsic membrane properties of locomotor network neurons in the lamprey spinal cord.* (Dissertation.) Stockholm, Sweden: Karolinska Institutet.

Watson, J. D.; Crick, F. H. C. 1953. Genetical implications of the structure of deoxyribonucleic acid. *Nature* **171**:954–7.

Wide-Swensson, D. 1994. *Hypertension in pregnancy. Effects of calcium channel blockade.* (Dissertation.) Lund, Sweden: University of Lund.

Wik, A. 2008. *When the rubber meets the road. Ecotoxicological hazard and risk assessment of tire wear particles.* (Dissertation.) Gothenburg, Sweden: The Sahlgrenska Academy of Gothenburg University.

Zdyb, A. M. 2008. *Jasmonates in root nodule development.* (Dissertation.) Stockholm, Sweden: Karolinska Institutet.

Index

Photo
>   a realistic view, 55
>   of a child, 74
>   ask a professional photographer, 56
>   concealing patient's anonymity,
>   74
>   of a human being, 74

Pie chart, 58

Plagiarism, 19

Quotations
>   from famous persons, 23

Referring, 38

Research letters, 37

Results
>   refer specialists to individual
>   papers, 57
>   synthesize data, 57

Sandwich format
>   definition, 4
>   versus Scandinavian model, 4

Scandinavian model
>   definition, 3
>   versus sandwich format, 3

Self-plagiarism, 19

Short reports, 37

Summary
>   popularized, 43

Supervisor, 85

Tables, 53

The Lancet, 37

Thesis,
>   definition, vii
>   at a glance, 25
>   differences from dissertaion, vii

Thesis by publication, 5

Three-dimensional graph, 63

Title
>   keywords, begin with, 15
>   main title, 14
>   neutral title, 16
>   subtitle, 14
>   with humor, 18
>   confusing title, 17
>   ending with a question mark,
>   16

US universities, 84

Watson, James D., 38

Writer's block, 45